Windows into Yesteryears

One man's search of truth and existence through a historical journey of his ancestral past

Lee Roy J. Pitre, Jr., AAS, BA, MS
(b.: 1960; 2-VIII-3-III-4-I-5-I-6-I-7-1-8-II-9-II-10-3-11-2)

Edited by
Leilya "Lilia" (Useinova) Pitre, AAS, BA, MA, Ph.D.

Original Publication 2014

Cover art, charts and maps, unless otherwise indicated,
by Lee Roy J. Pitre, Jr.

Acorn symbol on back cover:
Lee Roy Pitre, Sr.'s trade mark which he used when singing the back of fine furniture he built.
This one came from a custom designed bow and gun rack,
one of the last pieces of fine cabinets he built for me.

Inquiries and Reprints requests to
LeeRoy@Pitres.US

ISBN: (HardCover) 978-0-9904500-0-9
ISBN: (PaperBack) 978-0-9904500-1-6

A significant part of my inheritance is rooted in the genes of my ancestors. I have learned, adopted, and live by moral and ethical codes of my predecessors. I am who I am because of the family in which I was born and raised, because of my ancestral tree, and because of my education and life experiences. In the end, I answer for who I am, what I have done, what I have not done, but not for what others expect me to be.

Lee Roy J. Pitre, Jr.

Lee Roy James Pitre, Sr.
April 12, 1928 – October 14, 2006

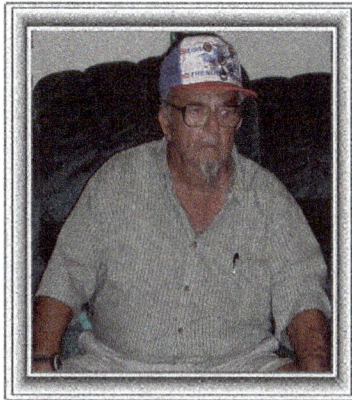

The culmination of my journey thus far
is dedicated to my Dad

Lee Roy J. Pitre, Sr. passed away at the age of 78 on October 14, 2006.

Fountain Memorial Gardens Cemetery in Lafayette, Louisiana.

Lee Roy James Pitre, Sr.   1928 - 2006

| 1942 | 1947 | 1952 | Mid 1950's | 1960 | 1990 | 2004 |

Table of Contents

SPECIAL ACKNOWLEDGEMENT

I would like to acknowledge Leilya "Lilia" (Useinova) Pitre, my loving wife and partner for supporting me through all the ups and downs of my journey and through countless hours of research and travel. She is a true loving and understanding partner who inspires me to go on with life and make the best of every moment. I am particularly grateful to the special couple that brought my Leilya into this world – Abdzhamil and Zore Useinov from Crimea, Ukraine.

Figure 1: Abdzhamil and Zore Useinov

I would also like to acknowledge those who donated a significant amount of their time towards assisting me with research and translations as well as their gracious hospitality:

Alan and Durline Melanson, Historical Association of Annapolis Royal, Canada;

Emily Neil, Researcher, Cajun French translations, Louisiana;

Fernand "Fern" Pitre, current owner of Claude Pitre's land of 1700

Roberta LeBoeuf Duplantis, Researcher, Cajun French translations, Louisiana;

Wayne Melanson, Interpretation Officer/Coordinator, Port-Royal National Historic Site, Canada.

ABOUT THIS BOOK

The information contained in this book is the fruition of many years of research and analysis by the author as well as many others. This book does not attempt to cover the entire history and lineage of all the Pitre's worldwide. It is only but an attempt at unlocking some of myths and facts of one person's ancestors, in addition to the origin of the surname "Pitre" by journeying into the past.

Since many of our ancestors have similar names, a superscript is added to each of the Pitre names. These superscripted $^{(A.b.nnnn;\ 1-I)}$ references indicate their generation and birth order. If the person is a direct ancestor of mine, it will start with an "A". The letters "b.nnnn" indicate the birth year and the Arabic number specifies generation, in which (1) begins with the first recorded Pitre to set foot in 15th century Acadia. The Roman numeral indicates order of birth for that generation. For example, Jean Pitre $^{(A.b.1636;\ 1-I)}$ means that Jean Pitre is a direct ancestor, born in 1636, first generation of the Pitres documented in North America. Since there are no official records, I assume he is the first born in that generation.

For the most part, I tried to keep things as chronological by year as I could. However, in some places I disrupted the chronological order to ease the understanding of subject matter, its relevancy, and readability. In many places, I digress from parents to their children and back as well as known associates, from one sibling to another and back.

Through many trips to governmental and historical society archives, court houses, libraries, and even Nova Scotia, I verified the information covered in this book from authenticated sources as much as it was feasible. In the case of personal interviews, the information has been corroborated from other sources. Therefore, there is no doubt this book contains both errors and omissions. I took great care in avoiding discussion groups, unsubstantiated opinions, and personal websites. To strengthen credibility of this research, all of the collected information was cross-referenced with multiple sources, including some primary sources. Therefore, researchers utilizing this book should not take the information in this book to be entirely factual despite my intent to keep it as accurate as possible.

In the event if a person's trade or occupation is listed or discussed within the book, it is based on the information originated from official government documents or from the first-hand documented interviews that have been corroborated.

Please, email errors, omissions, and comments to LeeRoy@Pitres.us. Submissions of official documents, photos, biography briefs, and historical narratives are most certainly welcomed for direct descendants of the Pitre bloodline since the years of 2014 and 2015 will find me hard at work researching additional leads for the second edition of the book.

ABOUT THE AUTHOR

Eleventh generation North American and seventh generation Louisianan

Lee Roy Pitre, Jr. [b.1960; 11-II][1] was born during the summer of 1960 in Lafayette, Louisiana. Lafayette is located in the southern central region of the state and is considered the heart of Cajun land.

He is the oldest son of Lee Roy J. Pitre, Sr. [A.b.1928; 10-III] and Lou Anna (Theriot) Pitre. His early years were spent in a modest two-bedroom house on the north side of the city. His father had purchased some land in the south of Lafayette that he had been farming for a few years prior to moving his family there in the summer of 1974.

Lee Roy's working career started in 1974 ... at the age of 13 working 50 hours a week during summers for $1 per hour as a carpenter apprentice. The apprenticeship lasted for five summers working alongside with his father.

Who could believe that a shy guy, who had barely graduated from high school in 1978, would end up with three university degrees and five technical diplomas? The path was long and difficult. Lee Roy, Jr. took classes at the University of Southwestern Louisiana[2] (which is now known as ULL) majoring in general business. He dropped out, attended a private trade school, earned a diploma in welding, and worked as welder building lift boats and barges. The spring of 1981 brought some new ambitions; he packed up and headed off to basic training in the US Air Force with high hopes of building a career in the medical field. Lee Roy graduated from basic training in May, 1981 and then completed Medical Services technical school. After three years of working in the Air Force hospital and taking various pre-med classes, in 1985 he found a new passion and decided to switch from a pre-med career path into computer science. Upon completion the Air Force's computer programming tech school in 1985, he was transferred to the Air Force Human Resources Laboratory in San Antonio, Texas.

In 1986, after many years of perseverance and changing paths, he earned his AAS in Data Processing from the Community College of the Air Force. Three years later, in 1989 he earned a BA in Computer Information Systems Management from Our Lady of the Lake University[3] in San Antonio, Texas. In 1994, Lee Roy received a Master of Science in Telecommunications degree from USL while working as the Computer Aided Information Systems coordinator for the College of Nursing.

---

[1] Lee Roy J. Pitre, Jr. [b.1960; 11-II] www.pitres.us
[2] University of Southwestern Louisiana "USL" (University of Louisiana at Lafayette "ULL") www.louisiana.edu
[3] Our Lady of The Lake University www.ollusa.edu

Another twist of the military service had happened in 1995 when Lee Roy was offered a direct commission as a medical service officer in the Louisiana Army National Guard[4] with the rank of the Second Lieutenant. He was thus assigned as Medical Platoon Leader with the Second Battalion 156 Infantry. In 1996, he completed the basic officer's course at the US Army Medical Academy at Fort Sam Houston, Texas. Being granted an early Medical Retirement as the First Lieutenant from the military in 1999, Lee Roy's heart and thoughts were and are always with the military, he holds a high pride for the free country and free will of the people living in it with strong emphasis on protecting individual rights and limiting power from oppressive governments.

The civil career introduces Lee Roy as a highly qualified programmer, analyst, and consultant. Every time his career takes the new turn, he gains more experience and extensive knowledge in various types of business lines. He has learned how to analyze technical progress and opportunities of computing business processes in many different areas of government, manufacturing, education and even insurance. Moreover, he is constantly searching for the answers to the questions about human lives and nature, just like this book, that is a result of more than 40 years of thinking, analyzing, and research.

---

[4] Louisiana Army National Guard http://www.la.ngb.army.mil/

A WORD FROM THE AUTHOR

The passing of my father, Lee Roy, Sr., on October 14, 2006, marked the closing of a significant chapter in his line of the Pitre family and my personal life. Everyone experiences death and reacts to it in his or her own way. I have seen death first hand many times while serving in the United States Air Force and witnessed the passing of the older relatives. I have even experienced loss on a very personal level when my best friend of 30 years decided to take his own life in 2001 while suffering from severe depression. However, none of those could be compared to the experiences immediately following my Dad's funeral. There is no other way of explaining it other than describing it as normal, weird, and enlightening at the same time.

The very first thing that I noticed the day after the funeral is that everyone immediately went on with their life as quickly as they could. It seemed almost like it never happened. Well, of course, that was not the case for me. It happened! He did exist! This is true because I'm here. I guess it is how everyone else chose to deal or not deal with their loss, or at least it feels that way to me. Maybe it was because of the daze I was in at the moment, and everything was going by very quickly instead of slowly. My first reaction was realization that simply moving on with my life was just not good enough. Therefore, my only recourse at the time was to escalate researching my heritage beginning from a mere curiosity to that of a professional inquiry with the intent of writing this book. I wanted to create a book that documents my journey back into the time of my ancestors' lives. It is kind of like peering out of the house through a window of discovery into the past. Hence, the name of my first book is *Windows into Yesteryears*.

There are many stories around about our ancestors. My father often told one story handed down to him by his father and grandfather. It was the story of two brothers with ancestral roots originated in France who immigrated to South Louisiana. Interview after interview, I would hear the same thing. The Pitre's of Louisiana came from France. Yet, a careful and detailed analysis of the facts would prove this is not exactly correct. My extensive research would uncover details of struggle, oppression, and opportunity that were unlike the stories passed down to me. Another story indicated that as far back as everyone could remember the Pitre's were descendants of a long line of ship builders. I would soon find out that the truth was somewhat different. I discovered that our ancestors belonged to a humble and proud lineage with a variety of occupations and spent most of their lives struggling just to survive. They made everything they needed with their own hands often bargaining for whatever else they needed. I was told that one of the brothers stayed in south Louisiana and the other migrated north, somewhere near present day Ville Plate. That is one story that has always intrigued me. However, although it is difficult to trace, that story had been proven by historical documents to be different from the truth. Growing up I often thought of those stories and over time came across others who had been told similar accounts. I often found myself pondering over numerous questions. We think we live in difficult political and economic times with increasing crime and poor performing schools. What was it really like back then? Who were our ancestors? What were their lives like? And how much of those stories were really true? What about all the stories I have never heard? Did traces of the truth survive the test of time and still exists today? How to find them and properly interpret within the factual context of their time?

Initially, I intended to stay away from stating in this book whether or not such stories were a fact or fiction. However, once I got into more detailed research, I found myself uncovering increasing amount of authenticated documents and verifiable stories. All that information contained clear clues and facts presenting themselves and shedding light to whether or not some of them were true. And, of course, I discovered many other details and surprising lessons along the way. After all, I am a realist. It is not an issue of rewriting history or one believing in what one wants history to be. Something either is or is not. As a professional analyst who believes in the power and wonders of science, my search for truth, who we are as humans, and where we really came from turn out to be one of the major things determining the purpose of my life. Striving to exclude information listed on discussion boards and people's ungrounded opinions and theories, I attempted to include mostly the information derived from official documents that I was able to track down and analyze over the years.

It is my intent to summarize and in some cases detail out the historical lives and major events of our ancestors. I am not determined to provide an analytical look at the research I have done nor validate or criticize the analysis of the others' research. Well, maybe just a little analysis and opinion. As humans, we cannot help it. However, no one can accurately provide a good objective analysis without sufficient solid facts. My research and analysis methods will surely bring out some criticism. My methodological approaches are based on what I know best and who I am. The many years of experience as an informational technology analyst and consultant as well as a military professional allow me to conduct this kind of research; however, it is a different type of career for me, and thus differs from the other genealogical research.

Based on various previous readings during my amateur research days, I firmly believed that authentic historical documentation about our Pitre ancestors prior to the 18th century was far and few, if existent at all. During those times, life was hard. Our ancestors were oppressed over and over again, exiled, ridiculed, and sometimes shunned. Yet, they maintained their pride because of who they were and where they came from despite all the challenges they encountered in life. From our present day concepts of life, it was almost unimaginable. In addition, at times the illiteracy rate was extremely high along with various language barriers that made survival even more challenging.

Initially, I had no idea where my journey in this endeavor would lead me. I only knew it was one I needed to undertake with a passion I had not felt since the birth of my daughters. For I knew, I could not really put the passing of my father behind me and go on with my life until I did. I had to gather what little information remained and document it before I also become merely a whisper in the wind. I longed to leave this legacy behind to be available to the future generations of the Pitre's.

Once I started researching from a professional point of view, I quickly discovered I was partly wrong. A treasure grove of historical documentation and information about the lives and times of the Pitre's does exist.

PROLOGUE

The first known person to be granted title "Pîtres" was Roger de Pîtres[5]. He was born during 1035 AD in Pîtres, Eure, Haunte-Normandie, France.

Although family names started being used in China around 2852 BC, it was not until the end of the Middle Ages that surnames became well established in Europe. Prior to the 10th century, European family names were practically non-existent. The concept of using surnames developed and evolved over time in a variety of forms and for a variety of reasons.

Surnames became more frequently used in western countries after the Norman invasions. It was during that time when the locations of castles in the regions around France became associated with surnames. Initially, surnames were not tied to an entire family and passed down. The words were granted as titles to such individuals as descriptors for financial or political reasons. If a Lord or Baron owned land or castle, he would have that area added to his name indicating the land included among his title. Eventually, surnames were used more for administrative reasons because of European expansion during the 1400's through 1600's due to increase in trade across regions. Some Norman, French, and Dutch surnames used habitational prefixes such as De. Historically, "De" signified ownership of lands and traditionally implied a mark of prestige. In comparison, "De" in Italian, French, Spanish, and Portuguese sometimes indicated a region of origin or sign of nobility.

It was during the 1400s that the use of surnames to identify a family started becoming popular in Europe. Initially it began with upper classes and then slowly spread out because of popularity and ease of identifying individuals. The surnames became more used as traveling merchants increased in number and geographical origin. With the growth of populations and commerce, it became gradually more difficult to specifically identify who owed whom. At that time, most people did not know or care whether some sort of descriptive name was attached to their name, nor was the same description used with each transaction. During 1450s names were still evolving and not always fixed. Most of the upper ranks had some sort of fixed, hereditary surname. Eventually, King Henry VIII (1491–1547) ordered that all marital births be recorded under the surname of the father.

Spelling of some names in past are assumed to be a deliberate choice. That could be explained by low literacy rates and incorrect translations due to significant number of dialects during travel or migration. Many people could not read or write, much less provide accurate spelling. So the scribe, clerk, minister, or other official would write down the name the way it was spoken. In addition, even the pronunciation was different depending on a dialect the person spoke.

Due to the significant number of dialects, illiteracy rate, and true meaning of slang of the times during the middle ages, the original meaning of some names may no longer be obtainable in modern English. Although many modern given and surnames are of a vast meaning an origin, most early European names are either of patronymic, toponymic, or occupational surnames. The methodology that was used to create surnames usually depended on the area.

As with many traditions, someone's lineage was determined by whom one's father was. There were some exceptions. In the middle ages, when a man of lower social status would marry a woman of higher status, he would often take on the wife's family name. Sometimes, lower class family names were changed or replaced by individuals to hide from crimes, political, or religious

---

[5] Roger de Pîtres, http://www.geni.com/people/Roger-de-Pitres-Sheriff-of-Gloucester/6000000001370540372

persecution. In England names usually came from someone's trade, for example, "Michael the Carpenter, "Richard the Thatcher", "John the Mason," or "James the Turner". In some cases, appearance would play a role in the adoption of a surname such as; Bald, Long, Short, Whitehead, Young.

In most of Europe, family names evolved from some feature of the person, such as their occupation, place of origin, or the social status of their parent's. "Robert Smith" would sometimes be short for "Robert the Smith," "Mary Windsor" for "Mary of Windsor," "Mark Johnson" short for "Mark, son of John," John Robert's son became John Robertson, "Richard Freeman" from "Richard the Freeman," and so on.

In the regions in and around Normandy and France, toponymic names were more common. Toponymic names, sometimes referred to as place names, were the ones that derived as descriptions of geographical locations. A name derived from a place or region can have many different origins. Sometimes as simple as symbolic in nature or the thought or emotion a person experienced the first time when encountering the region. Often, it was geographical in origin, such as: Bridge, Camp, Hill, Bush, Lake, Wood, Grove, Forest, Fields, or Stone. In some cases, descendants of land-owners chose to be known by their holdings; castle, manor, or estate, e.g., Elmer, Windsor, Staunton.

Figure 2 : 5th Century Europe

One specific example of a place name that is at the heart of my journey has but rarely referenced in western literature is *Pîsters*. An early reference is in one of Marie De France's[6] lays *A*

[6] Marie De France, http://archive.org/stream/mariedefrancesev00mari/mariedefrancesev00mari_djvu.txt

Tale of Two Lovers, in a distant land from a time long past. It refers to a story of how a sixth century King who was lord over the lands gave dedication over a little valley in honor of a suitor to his beloved daughter. Thus, the valley was dedicated to the *Pîsters* people. *Pîsters* is a word considered to be from an ancient Franco dialect. At the time, the country of France, as we know it today, did not exist. The mountain that Marie De France described in her tale actually exists. It is near the commune of Pîtres in the Haute-Normandie region of France.

The city of *Pîtres*[7], as it is known today still exists in central Normandy. My research has not uncovered who exactly was that 6th century King. Perhaps it was King Clovis. However, various translations sometimes refer to him as King of *Pîstrians* or one who rules over the *Pîsters* people. During the 5th and early 6th centuries, the Visigoths ruled a large kingdom in the southern region of France. In 507, Clovis[8] (King of the Franks) defeated Euric's son north of Poitiers. The French territory of the Visigoths was reduced to a coastal strip. This proves that in the fifth and sixth centuries the territory known as modern France represented various regions that were ruled and occupied by different peoples.

In 525 AD, we find a historical reference to the founding of Merovingian house *Pîtres* by Merovingian Kings[9]. At that time, it was under English noble rule. In a slightly different dialect, *Pîstus* appears in 660AD[10], in a diploma of Clotaire III in favor of the abbey of Chelles. In 885, the Viking conquest up the Seine River to Paris was temporarily halted by the defenses at Pitres. Historically, it had a bridge to prevent Vikings from sailing up the river to Paris. It was there that King Charles the Bald promulgated the Edict of *Pîstres* in 864. For a variety of reasons, history has recorded the word's spelling in different ways: *Pîstres* during pre-Medieval period, Pîstrians later, and eventually, *Pîtres* in modern France.

The author believes that the origin of *Pîsters* is more likely to be a description of people in a specific geographical location of northern present day France in the pre-medieval ages. The city of *Pîtres* is located in the southeastern Normandy area. It is a rather small city that sits along the northern bank of the Seine River, about 30 miles southeast of the city of Rouen. Throughout European history, it was of little significance to the world. However, it did play an important role in history. According to the recorded history, it is a commune[11] which helped block Vikings' incursions up the Seine River to Paris during Charles the Bald's reign[12]. It is especially significant to my journey because it seems to be the geographical origin of the *Pitre* family name.

Just because the word "*Pîsters*" is a reference to medieval Franco and early Normandy when those areas were under English control, it does not mean everyone living in the Normandy and Flanders […modern day northern France and southern Belgium…] areas are of French or English descent. It is more likely that many were of Dutch and Viking descent.

During the late 12th Century, the Norman dukes paid homage to the King of France. Before the fall of the fortress Château-Gaillard, Normandy was not a part of the Kingdom of France, so early *Pîtres* were not really considered to be inside the kingdom of France. In fact, France was not yet considered to be a single country.

---

[7] *Pîtres* http://en.wikipedia.org/wiki/P%C3%AEtres
[8] King Clovis of the Franks http://www.historyworld.net
[9] Merovingian house Pîtres http://www.angelfire.com/journal2/ck15endtimecolumn/et9.html
[10] Jean-Carles EBRO ebro.liliane@neuf.fr,
[11] Commune http://en.wikipedia.org/wiki/Communes_of_France
[12] King Charles II, http://www.britannica.com/EBchecked/topic/106851/Charles-II, http://www.france.fr/en/outstanding-men-and-women/charles-ii-bald-823-877.html

Historians believe the words "Flanders" and "Flemish" are derived from Frisian and Germanic most likely meaning overflow or flooding. The earliest known reference to the Flemish people is from Saint Eligius biography (ca. 590-660)[13]. The country of Flanders existed from 862 until 1795 AD.

Providing the above information, I do not intend to draw a direct link between the ancestors of Jean (Jehan) Pitre (1636) and the Nobles of Pîtres (Pîstrians) from the third through 14th century. What I offer here is the documentation of the word Pîtres (latter Pitre) as toponymic in its historic origin and specifically a description of a geographical location initially dedicated around the third and fourth centuries. Many people took on the surname of *Pîsters,* Pîtres, and eventually Pitre, all of which indicating of the village of *Pîsters*, now known as Pîtres. The vast majority of Pîtres are not necessarily descendants of nobility. However, discovering the ancestry origin in the region is perhaps far more than coincidence, and it explains how the last name came to existence.

THE JOURNEY

This journey, like many other journeys in human history, is driven by two age old questions "What" and "Why." These questions have motivated countless others throughout the human history in innumerable other expeditions to satisfy their quest for enlightenment.

As stated in the opening, this book is dedicated to Lee Roy J. Pitre, Sr. [A.b.1928; 10-3] as well as his lineage that preceded him. A hardy line of descendants went through it all—wars, exportation, exile, poverty, and natural disasters—continues to survive and in many cases thrives. It is a story of persistence and determination without giving up that began with the descendants of the two people who left an oppressive Europe to live in a mid-17th century North American colony. Their offspring had increased to the hundreds of thousands during the 21st century.

Who knows the truth of the times? Do we even understand the truth of our very complex postmodern society, much less that of our ancestors? What were people's lives really like in the distant past? We can only relate our successes and struggles during contemporary times to our imagination of how people coped and survived during the 1600s through the introduction of modern medicine and technology. This is not to mention the unfairness of justice system of the time compared to what we benefit currently and have come to demand.

Today, with so many luxuries and the endless opportunities our rights and freedoms offer, many people are struggling to fit in and be part of a group still preserving their individualities. It is not so hard to imagine from that point of view that "fitting in" was even more important during the early American colonial days. Individualism was much riskier without being noticed. People were constantly struggling with the dilemma between how their governments wanted to rule over them versus how those people wanted to live and prosper. Evidently, at that time more so than now, they really did not want to be noticed with all the turmoil and battles between rival countries. They simply wanted to live their lives from day to day in the only way they could. Many consider that along with the high level of illiteracy that is directly related to the lack of historical documentation of how many people lived and where they came from. As part of other discoveries, this is not necessarily the case.

Why were so many people willing to leave behind everything and everyone they were familiar with, cross over a vast ocean, not even knowing if they would survive the trip to a new, unknown wilderness half a world away? To some, it was the promise of vast amounts of land they could claim as their own. To others, it was an attempt to leave behind the oppressive governments and culture that extensively controlled their lives and religious beliefs. And yet, there were ones who were perhaps trying to escape some aspects of their past life while others were criminals with little options and chose to risk the promises of a new life in a new land.

THE EARLY ACADIAN COLONIES

Jean Pitre [A.b:1636; I] is my eighth great-grandfather. Of the few documents that survived from the mid-17th century, he is believed to be the first Pitre ancestor who settled in North America. It is not known when he arrived in L'Acadie, known now as Nova Scotia, Canada, or if he was born there. He spent most of his life in and around the 17th century French colony known as *Port Royal*, present day town of Annapolis Royal. It is located along the southern bank of the Annapolis River.

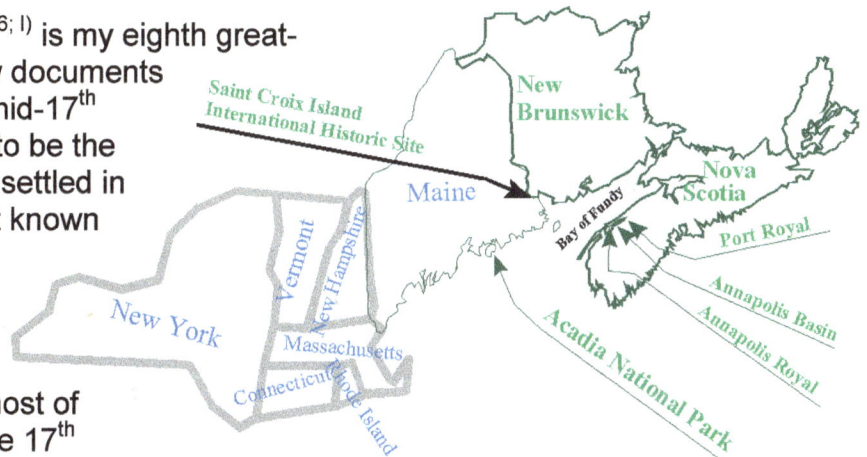

Acadia, as it is now referred to, was originally pronounced *L'Acadie* by the early French, Scottish, and Dutch settlers. It includes the areas inhabited by the French and Scottish settlers around the Bay of Fundy and eventually Île Saint-Jean and Île Royale. Over time, those settlers became known as "*The Acadians*". Out of all the known exiles and conquered nations, it is believed that the Acadians are the only ones who most accurately retained their original customs and beliefs over the centuries up to the present days. All other displaced cultures and traditions were eroded or assimilated to the dominating cultures over time.

In1604, early French explorers picked a small island on the Rivière Dauphin. They built their first permanent settlement there – along the present day Saint Croix River between Maine and New Brunswick in Nova Scotia. That same year they would discover the error of their decision after experiencing the bitter cold winters of the north eastern Americas. That winter, with limited resources on the island, nearly half of the original 79 colonist paid the ultimate price and died of scurvy, a disease resulting from a deficiency of vitamin C.

During the spring of 1605, while searching for a more suitable location, they befriended the Mi'kmaq people along present day Annapolis River. The Mi'kmaq people were resourceful and welcoming; they had settled the region thousands of years earlier. That new settlement was located on the north bank of the Annapolis River, near the contemporary Habitation reconstruction site. Learning from their previous mistakes, the survivors built a fort. There they were better sheltered from the harsh winters with abundant supply of food and trees. This became one the first permanent European settlement in North America. Thus, they christened their new home "Port Royal".

During the fall of 1613, the inhabitants left their shelter unattended as they often did while they were tending to their traps up river. Samuel Argall led a group of English, attacked and destroyed the colony after looting it. After loading their boats with the spoils they looted, the Englishmen burned the habitation to the ground prior to departure. Argall was from the Virginia colony and was commissioned to expel all French from North American territories. The habitation was thus abandoned and most of the trappers returned to Europe. A few that had taken Mi'kmaq wives decided to stay and were scattered throughout the area.

Figure 3 : Port Royal Habitation (re-creation)

Around1632, a new French and Scottish settlement was established five miles upstream on the southern bank where present day Annapolis Royal is. It was also initially named Port Royal and renamed to Annapolis Royal in 1710 when it was seized by English forces.

Figure 4 : Port Royal Census of 1671[14]

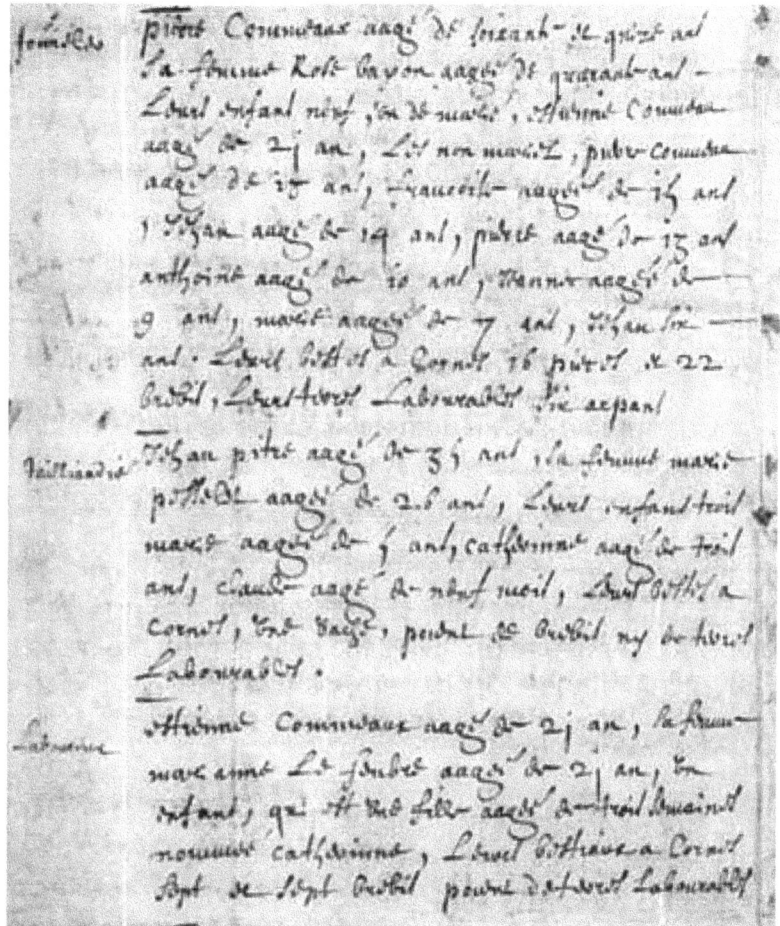

During the mid-17th century, one of those early Acadian settlers was known as Jean Pitre [(A.b:1636; I)]. No one knows for sure where he was born. It is estimated that Jean was born around 1636 according to census data collected in the late 1600s. Very limited information can be found about him during the mid to later 1600s. According to the 1671 census, he was 35 and married to Marie Pesseley. Marie Pesseley was the youngest child of Isaac and Barbe Pesseley. She was born in 1645. Based on the ages of the children from the census, they were married around 1665 in Port Royal. Documents from the time state that Marie's parents were from France. They had arrived in *L'Acadia* some 30 years earlier aboard the ship *Saint Jean* on April 1, 1636 from La Rochelle, France. Marie's mother returned to France after her father was killed in 1645 at Fort Saint Jean. According to Jean [(A.b:1636; I)] and Marie's grandson, Claude Marc Pitre, Marie was born in Paris, and Jean [(A.b:1636; I)] is of Flemish descent.

Jean's occupation was listed in an early census as "taillandier", which some translate as edge-tool maker. Therefore, it is commonly assumed he provided for his family by sharpening or making tools. In 1671, he did not own any land according to the census. However, he did own one cow. By 1678, Jean declared that he owned two cows and two arpents of land further up the river. He also stated that his land was

---

[14] 1671 Census, MIKAN no. 2319362, http://collectionscanada.gc.ca/pam_archives/index.php?fuseaction=genitem.displayItem&rec_nbr=2319362

under cultivation. An arpent is a term of the time used to describe a parcel of land, a pre-metric French length unit. The unit had various standards of measurement associated with arpents at the time. The most common measure was 180 feet used in North America. In Europe, it referred to 220 feet. Knowing that Jean owned the land implied that the land was farmed.

There is no known documentation about Jean Pitre [A.b:1636; I] before the 1671 census. According to one Acadian historian and genealogist, Father Clarence d'Entremont speculates that Jean Pitre [A.b:1636; I] may have been a Peters from England. There was an account of a black smith by the name of John Peters coming over from England. However, as my research journey continued on, I realized that assumption did not seem plausible for that particular time due to several reasons.

Careful and detailed analysis of the relative locations of each homestead cross referenced with each census indicates that Jean's [A.b:1636; I] land was next to Pierre Comeau (the elder) located up river on the southern bank just west of *Pré Rond (Prée Ronde marsh)*. It was along the south river bank, just south of *Belleisle*. One must take extra care when analyzing the family settlements along the Annapolis valley, since multiple Comeau relatives had the same name as Pierre Comeau. Without additional documentation, it is difficult to determine if each of these Pierre Comeaus is a descendant of the elder or perhaps a cousin.

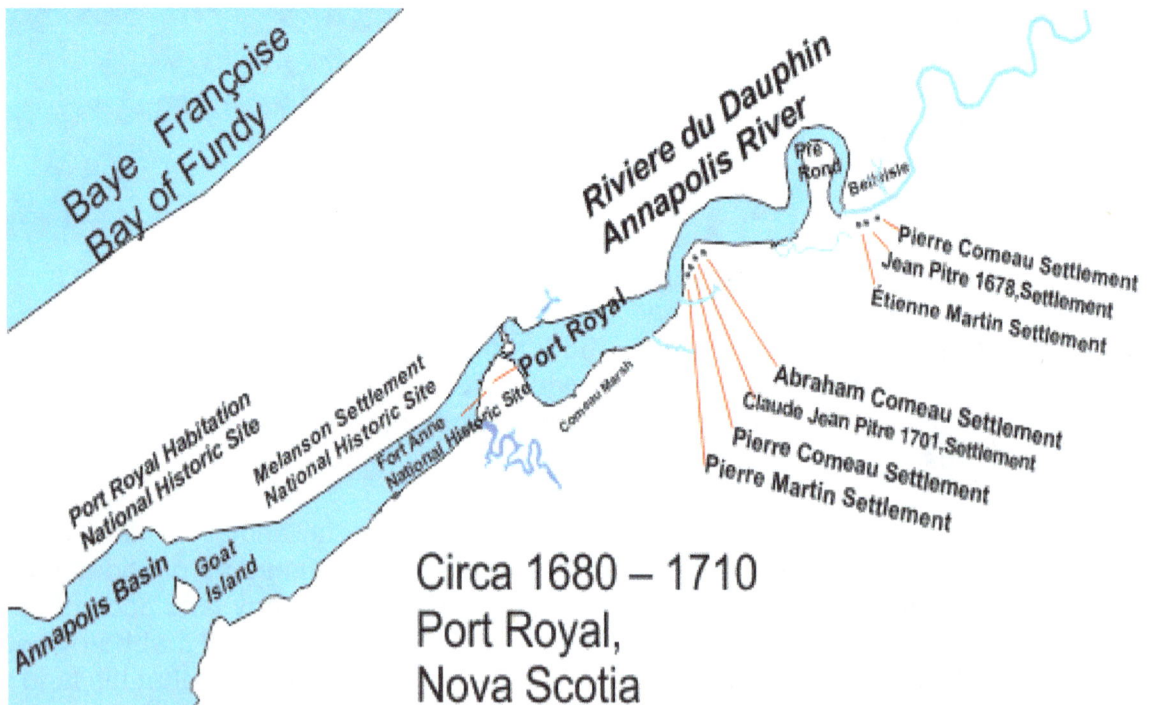

Figure 5 : Annapolis valley 1680 - 1710

The Early Acadian Colonies

There is a map entitled "Au Coeurs de l'Acadie" of family homesteads plotted along the "Riviere Dauphin". It was published around 1987 by Annapolis Ventures and was based in part on census data. The map was originally drawn by Léopold Lanctôt. An enhanced version of the 1707 representation map was commissioned by the Centre of Geographic Sciences, Human Resources Development of Canada. It was plotted after detailed analysis of various census and other documents. During my visit to the Annapolis valley, I found that different size copies can be purchased at the Fort Anne gift shop as well as at museum in Grand Pre.

One of the younger Pierre Comeaus settled on the peak of the highest hill between the river and the western end of where current day Marsh road is located. Jean's [A.b:1636; I] first born son, Claude Jean Pitre [b.1671; 2-III], would later settle here after marrying the younger daughter of Pierre Comeau, Anne Comeau. Also it is necessary to be careful considering the 1701 census of the family at this same location. Jean [A.b:1636; I] had already passed away by 1688. It states "Jean Pitre", when it should have stated "Claude Pitre". Some people believe that was an indication that Claude inherited the property from his father. That does not appear plausible since Jean's homestead was much further up river. Perhaps, Jean was Claude's [b.1671; 2-III] middle name. However, it was Claude Pitre [b.1671; 2-III], married to Anne Comeau who was helping with her father's homestead.

1680s

By the time the 1686 census took place, Jean's [A.b:1636; I] family had grown to seven children. The two eldest daughters had marred and were homesteading along the Annapolis valley with their new families. Jean [A.b:1636; I] was 53 years old when he died around 1688. By then, Jean and Marie had 11 children: Marie [b.1666], Catherine [b.1668], Claude Jean [b.1671], Marc [b.1673], infant Pitre [b.1675] (died young), Pierre [b.1677], Jean Denis [A.b:1680], Francois [b.1682], Marguerite [b.1683], and Jeanne [b.1685]. Four of their daughters married into the Amireau dit Tourangeau, Bertrand, Comeau, and Piat dit La Bonté families.

After Jean's [A.b:1636; I] death, Marie Pesseley left the family farm and returned to live in the town of Port Royal. There she married Francois Robin and finished raising her children at his residence across the street from Fort Anne. My belief is that she sold the property back to her neighbor Pierre Comeau (the elder). Jean's [A.b:1636; I] youngest son, Jean Denis [A.b:1680; 2-VII], was my seventh great-grandfather. He was also the seventh child born to Jean [A.b:1636; I], and Marie.

1690s

I do not know for sure why Jean Denis [A.b.1680; 2-VII] and his brother Pierre [b.1677; 2-VI] did not settle as farmers and decided to move further northwest up the river valley. However, it is likely that either they were not interested in farming or simply trying to get further away from the turmoil between the English and French wars. In either case, Pierre Thibodeau recruited Jean [A.b.1680; 2-VII] and his brother Pierre [b.1677; 2-VI] around 1698. They assisted with the construction of a new flourmill at Chipoudy, now known as Shepody, New Brunswick, Canada. Pierre Thibodeau founded Chipoudy around 1698 with his four sons and Guillaume Blanchard. The village was located on the northwest side of Chipoudy Bay. During that time, Jean Denis [A.b.1680; 2-VII] returned to Port Royal to marry Francoise Babin, the tenth child of Antoine Babin and Marie Mercier (French-born Acadians).

The original village name of Cobequid was derived from the Mi'kmaq word *wagobagitk*, meaning the *bay runs far up.* It is commonly believed that at the time they were referring to the area surrounding the eastern inlet of Minas Basin.

THE 18TH CENTURY

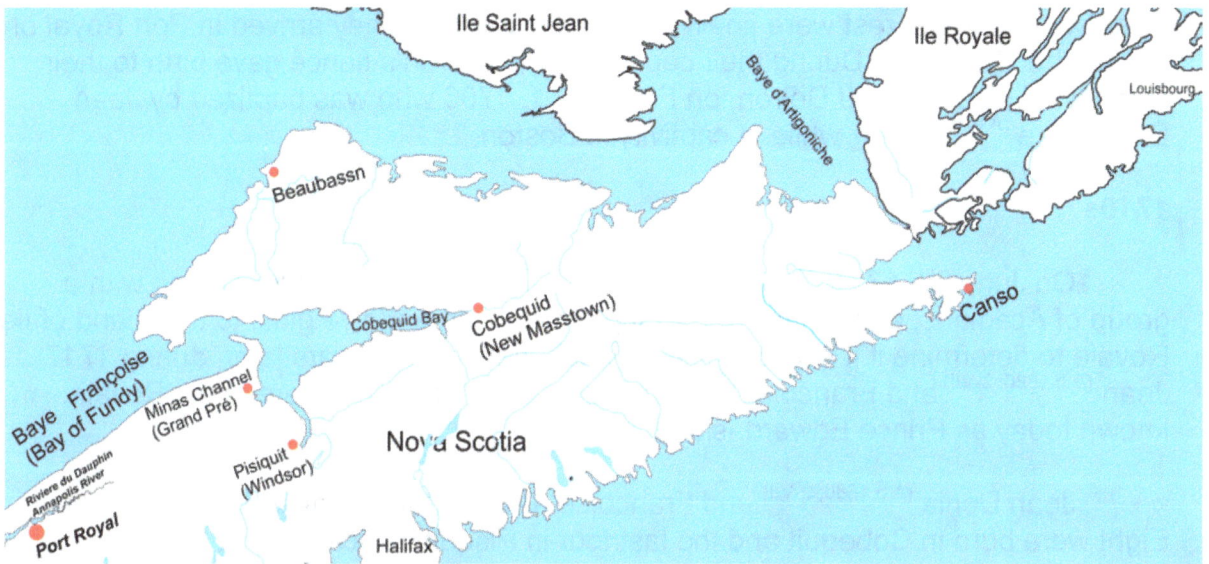

1700s

Since the new mill was running by autumn of 1700 in Chipoudy, Canada, Jean Denis Pitre [(A.b.1680; 2-VII)] decided to settle his new family there on the upper west side of Chipoudy Bay (now Shepody Bay). According to the census of Rivière-de-l'Ascension conducted in 1701 at Les Mines, it lists Jean Denis [(A.b.1680; 2-VII)] and Francoise Pitre's family of four which included their two sons – Jean [(b.1699; 3-I)] and Joseph [(b.1700; 3-II)]. Both were born in Cobequid. It also stated that Jean Denis [(A.b.1680; 2-VII)] had one gun, nine cattle, six sheep, and five hogs on five arpents of land. Therefore, it seems that he was relatively prosperous at the time. Their third son, Claude Jean [(A.b.1701; 3-III)] was born later that year. Claude Jean [(A.b.1701; 3-III)] was my sixth great-grandfather.

Jean Denis [(A.b.1680; 2-VII)] and Francoise resettled several times. Within two years, they had relocated to Beaubassin, and by 1708 they were in Cap Sable.

According to correspondence with Marie Henry, Noel Doiron's wife, Jean Denis [(A.b.1680; 2-VII)] was even living in Boston, Massachusetts, for a short period of time. He was held there along with other Acadians as prisoners from Major Benjamin Church in the Raids of 1704. During the Queen Anne's war in July 1704, Major Benjamin Church conducted raids in retaliation for the Deerfield, Massachusetts massacre. His raids included the coastline of Maine, Saint Stephen, New Brunswick, Grand Pre, Pisquit, and Chignecto. He boasted of having left only five houses standing and took

---

The 18th Century   Page 29 o

45 Acadians as prisoners back to Boston. Noel Doiron was one of the prisoners taken during the raid of Pisquit. There they roamed the streets of Boston freely while awaiting France to pay ransom. A group was eventually returned to L'Acadie in 1705. After two years, the rest were finally returned to Acadia. They arrived in Port Royal on September 18, 1706. During their captivity, Noel Doiron's fiancé gave birth to their first child, Louis Mathieu Doiron, on February 1, 1706 who was baptized by Jean Denis Pitre [(A.b.1680; 2-VII)] while in captivity in Boston.

1710s

On June 28, 1714 Jean Denis Pitre [(A.b.1680; 2-VII)] took his family along with a group of Acadians, at that time consisting of five boys and five girls, to the island of Île Royale to determine if it was suitable for habitation. A few years later, during 1717 Jean [(A.b.1680; 2-VII)] and Francoise (Babin) were still living somewhere on Île Royale, known today as Prince Edward Island.

Jean Denis [(A.b.1680; 2-VII)] and Francoise had 12 children over a 26-year span. Eight were born in Cobequit and the last four in Pisquit, indicating that he moved to Pisquit sometime around 1712. They probably died somewhere in L'Acadie. There is no record of the couple boarding any ships during the expulsions. Many of their children were not so fortunate. Their eldest son Jean Baptiste and his wife, Marguerite Theriot, died at sea during the crossing to France from Île Saint Jean. Their daughter Madeleine and her husband (Louis Mathieu Doiron, whom Jean had 'baptized' in Boston) died in during the shipwreck of Duke Williams along with their other son Joseph and his wife, and his grandson Michel with wife. Their daughter Cecile and her husband died in the shipwreck of the Violet. Their son Germain and his wife died somewhere in the West Indies.

1720s

Around 1724 Claude Jean Pitre [(A.b.1701; 3-III)], my sixth great grandfather, married sixteen-year-old Marguerite Doiron in Cobequid. She was the daughter of Noel Doiron and Marie Henry. They had eight children over 22 years. Two of Claude Jean's siblings would marry two of Marguerite's siblings.

Claude Jean [(A.b.1701; 3-III)] and Marguerite's first child was born within a year of their marriage. Benjamin Pitre [(A.b.1725; 4-I)] was my fifth great-grandfather and was born in Cobequit. He was followed by seven brothers.

1730s

This section intentionally left blank pending additional research.

1740s

By 1746 Claude Jean Pitre [(A.2-VII-3-III)] and Marguerite had eight children. Seven of them were born in Cobequit, Acadia: Benjamin [(A.b.1725)], Claude [(b.1727)], Jean Baptiste [(b.1729)], Paul Hypolite [(b.1732)], Francois [(b.1734)], Raphael [(b.1739)], and Olivier [(b.1741)]. Only Ambroise [(b.1746)] born on Île Royale.

About 1747 Benjamin [(A.b.1725; 4-I)] married Jeanne Moyse. Jeanne was the eldest daughter born at Port Royal of Francois Moyse and Marie Brun. Benjamin and Jeanne had a son, Canute, and two daughters Agnes and Francoise, before the expulsion of Acadians by the English began. That expulsion, as for so many other families, became an ill-fated journey for the Pitres. Jeanne Moyse died at sea during the crossing. Benjamin [(A.b.1725; 4-I)] would later meet and marry his second wife, which would become my fifth great-grandmother during his exile in France.

1750s

Both Claude Jean [(A.b.1701; 3-III)] and Marguerite possibly died before or during the deportations. There is no documentation proving that they sought refuge or resettled elsewhere.

By, 1755, Benjamin [(A.b.1725; 4-I)] and Jeanne had three children together. They were eventually captured and expelled during 1758.

Le Grand Dérangement (1755-1758)

It is a common misconception that all Acadians were deported from Port Royal in 1755. The documentation suggests that only around 6,000 of Nova Scotia's 12,000 to 18,000 Acadians were removed during the initial phase of the Grand Dérangement of 1755. They were exiled from Port Royal, Grand Pre, and Beaubassin to American colonies and England.

Many thousands managed to escape and made their way to Île St-Jean (now known as Prince Edward Island). At that time, it was under the French rule. By 1758, approximately 3,000 to 5,000 Acadians were residing on the island. After the fall of Louisburg on the neighboring Cape Brenton Island in 1758, Île Saint-Jean was

Figure 6 : 1st Exportation Site, Pier in Port Royal

then occupied by British forces. Between September and November of that year, another 2,200 Acadians were removed using 16 ships destined for France.

Exportations at Île Saint Jean went slowly. Soon after their departure, some ships were delayed in the Gut of Canso (known as Strait of Canso) until November 25, 1758. About 3,500 Acadians were deported in 1758. Many did not survive the trip. Two ships sank. From the ones who were deported from Île Saint Jean, 1,650 either drowned or died of disease.

Ten ships reached St. Malo from Île Royale and Île St.-Jean in late 1758 and early 1759 with a total death rate of almost 50% (including en route and after arrival), not counting Violet and Duke Williams.

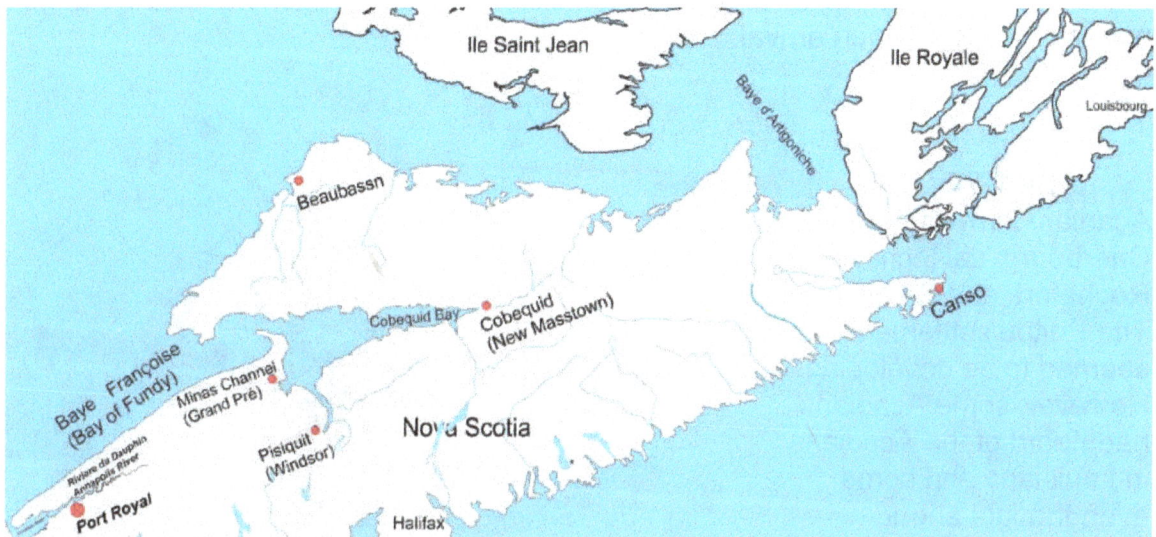

Four of Claude Jean [(A.b.1701; 3-III)] and Marguerite sons, Claude [(b.1727; 4-II)], Paul [(b.1731; 4-IV)], Francois [(b.1734; 4-V)], and Raphael [(b.1739; 4-VI)], arrived in St. Malo from Cherbourg on 20th of July 1759. Younger brother Olivier [(b.1741; 4-VII)], his wife and children arrived in St. Malo from St. Pierre and Miquelon on 13th of November 1767 on the schooner La Creole. It is unknown what happened to Jean Baptiste [(b.1729; 4-III)].

Benjamin Pitre [(A.b.1725; 4-I)] and his family were loaded onto one of the ships known as "The Five". To date, no documents have been found detailing which Acadian sailed on which of the "Five Ships". What is known is the "Five ships" departed L'Acadie and arrived in St. Malo simultaneously. Only Benjamin [(A.b.1725; 4-I)] and his oldest daughter Agnes survived the crossing. They arrived at St. Malo on January 23, 1759. They lived in St. Suliac for the first six months and in La Gouesniere for the last six months of 1759. It was at La Gouesniere where Benjamin [(A.b.1725; 4-I)] married again to Marguerite Boudrot, a woman about 15 years his junior. Marguerite was the daughter of Jean Baptiste Boudrot and Catherine Brassaud. They settled in St. Suliac where their first five children were born: Marie [(b.1781; 5-IV)], Madeleine Modeste [(b.1763; 5-V)], Jean Baptiste [(b.1765; 5-VI)], Cecile Olive [(b.1768; 5-VIII)], and Marguerite Charlotte [(b.1770; 5-IX)].

1760s

Belle-Ile-en-Mer was under English control when 78 Acadians families arrived there after expulsion from Nova Scotia in 1764. It was eventually returned to France in the treaty of 1762. Several of these families made declarations of their heritage and ancestor's origins upon arrival.

1770s

By 1770s, 586 Acadians arrived at Cherbourg, LaRochelle, Rochefort, and St. Malo. The Poitou settlement seemed to be developing. However, some Acadians had heard of the Acadians in Louisiana and some even thought about resettling in the Sierra Morena of Spain. But the Minister strongly opposed both ideas.

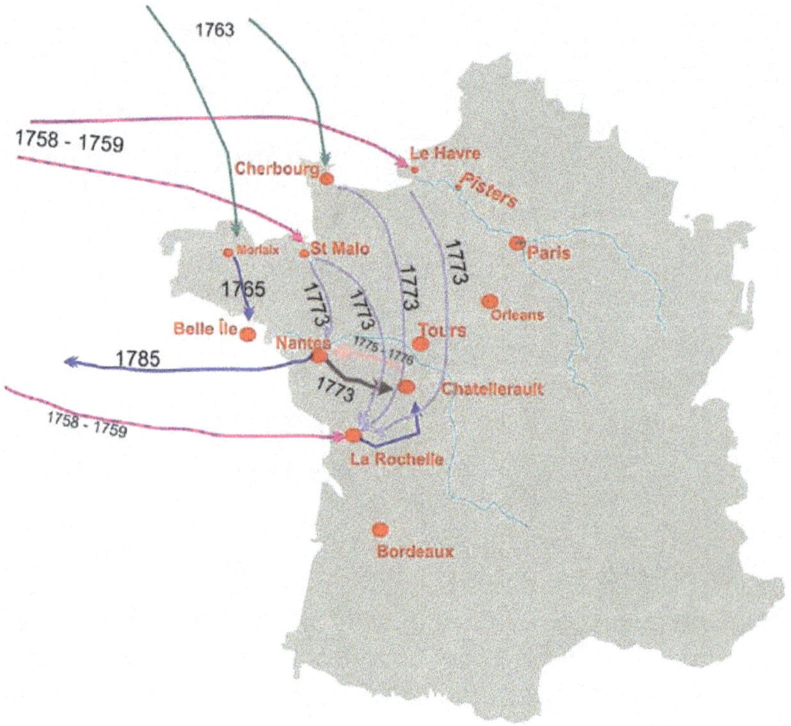

While the Acadians were waiting for more money to help the settlement, eight Acadian families secretly moved from St. Malo to Jersey Island. At the time, the census listed 1,727 Acadians in the area. The last major migration of Acadians leaving St. Malo area was in 1785 when 316 Acadians left for Louisiana aboard the *Ville d'Arcangel*.

Figure 7 : Acadians Exile in France 1700s

A census conducted on September 15, 1772 listed Benjamin [A.b.1725; 4-I] as 45 years old and a little deranged. It also listed his second wife, Marguerite Boudrot, indicating spinning and sewing as her occupation.

Following the birth of the next two children, Francois Jean [b.1773] and Genevieve Louise [b.1775], Benjamin [A.b.1725; 4-I] and Marguerite's family now adding up to nine persons were documented as being relocated in the fourth convoy leaving Chatellerault France for Nantes (6 March –13 March 1776). At Nantes, Benjamin's [A.b.1725; 4-I] eldest daughter Agnes married Joseph Guerin.

1780s

By 1783 Benjamin $^{(A.b.1725; 4-I)}$ and Marguerite had 10 children together. Marie Pitre $^{(b.1761; 5-IV)}$, Madeleine Modeste $^{(b.1763; 5-V)}$, Jean Baptiste Pitre $^{(v.1765; 5-VI)}$, Cecile Olive Pitre $^{(b.1768; 5-VII)}$, Marguerite Charlotte Pitre $^{(b.1770; 5-VIII)}$ 01/25/1770; Francois Jean Baptiste Pitre $^{(b.1773; 5-IX)}$, Genevieve Louise Pitre $^{(b.1775; 5-X)}$, Etienne Pitre $^{(b.1778; 5-XI)}$, Jean Francois Pitre $^{(A.b.1780; 5-XII)}$, and Mathurin Pitre $^{(b.1783; 5-XIII)}$.

Jean Francois Pitre $^{(A.b.1780; 5-XII)}$ is my fourth great-grandfather. He was born on October 2, 1780 in St. Pierre de Reze, Bretagne, France, and died between1813-1832 in Ascension, LA.

Benjamin Pitre $^{(A.b.1725; 4-I)}$ died on September 30, 1782 in St Pierre de Reze, Bretagne, France.

The Acadian Migration from France to Louisiana of 1785

In the later part of the 1700s, the Spanish were attempting to settle their territory along the western bank of the Mississippi River in the North America. They had constructed the post of La Fourche during the mid-1700s at the junction of Bayou LaFourche and Mississippi river. Around 1770, a Catholic chapel was constructed in the post and was referred to as the Parochial church of Assumption. At that time, the full name of the church as La Iglesia de La Ascension de Nuestro Señor Jesu Christo De la Fourche de los Chétimachae. The area was referred to as "La Paroisse de l'Ascension". Hence the reference in various birth certificates in French and later English as "Parish of Ascension of La Fourche".

In the 1778, the Spanish also established a military post along upper Bayou LaFourche and called it Valenzuela. It was located just south of its intersection with the Mississippi river near present day Belle Alliance.

The Bell Alliance plantation was located on the east bank of Bayou LaFourche about five miles east of Donaldsonville. The initial 7,000 acre plot of land was granted during the 1770s to Don Juan Vives, a Spanish military physician.

Despite all their efforts, the Spanish where having trouble encouraging more Spanish to come and help settle the area. In 1779, at the Spanish King's expense they decided to sponsor resettlement of Isleños in the Valenzuela area between present day Donaldsonville and Plattenville. The Isleños were from Canary Island. But yet, that was still not enough non-British people in the area as a buffer between the British and Spanish territories.

Having heard of the poor treatment of the Acadian exiles in France by the French, Spain sent an envoy in secret to the western areas of France in attempts to solicit any Acadian interests. In effort to entice them into resettling, each family head was offered promises of a land grant and $32 (approximately $64,000 today). Eventually, Spain was so successful in luring the Acadians that they paid for seven ships to transport approximately 1,600 Acadians to the Spanish colony in the Louisiana territory. The seven ships were known as *Le Bon Papa*, *La Bergre*, *Le Beaumont*, *Le Satin-Remi*, *L'Amite*, *La Ville d'Archangel*, and *La Caroline*.

L'AMITIÉ

(18th century, 400 ton, three-masted frigate)

Captain Joseph Beitremieux

Acadian exodus from France to Louisiana 1785

Departed from La Rochelle, France, on August 20, 1785
Arrived in New Orleans, Louisiana, on November 8, 1785

VUE DU NAVIRE L'AMITIÉ

APARTENANT A MM. RATEAU

Figure 8 : Painting by Francois Geoffroy Roux (1811-1882)

Marguerite Boudrot [(A.b.1741)], Age 46, widow of Benjamin Pitre [(A.b1725;4-I)]

Upon arrival at New Orleans, the Acadians were more than welcomed. They were fed and housed there while the families made their decision as to where they wanted to settle.

Some went to Attakapas, Opelousas area, and north of Baton Rouge along Bayou des Ecores (present day Thompson's Creek), but most chose to settle along Bayou LaFourche area. Most who settled along Bayou des Ecores later decided to move to Bayou LaFourche.

In 1785, some Acadian families from France were also settled at "Valenzuela in La Fourche." As a result of the Spanish sponsoring of the Acadian resettlement, the land west of the Mississippi river became known as the second Acadian Coast.

One of those families was, Benjamin Pitre's [A.b.1725; 4-I] remaining family members departed France on August 20, 1785 on board the ship L'Amite. They arrived in New Orleans 80 days later on November 8, 1785. This small surviving family consisted of his widow Marguerite Boudrot [A.b.1741] now 46 years old, her children Marie[b.1761; 5-IV], 23, Magdelaine [b.1763; 5-V], 21, Cecille [b.1768; 5-VIII], 15, Marguerite [b.1770; 5-IX],14, Etienne [b.1778; 5-XII], 7, and Jean[b.1780; 5-XIII], 4. Agnes [b.1748; 5-I], Benjamin's first born daughter with his first wife Jeanne Moyse, and her family left France for Louisiana as well.

Shortly after arrival in New Orleans, Marguerite Boudrot [A.b.1741] decided to claim one of the Spanish land grants and settle along east bank of lower Bayou LaFourche. This area would later become known as the *Parish of Ascension* in the *District of La Fourche.*

Marguerite Boudrot's [A.b.1741] (my fifth great-grandmother) Spanish land grant of six arpents was a little further south of Valenzuela and present day Plattenville. Careful detailed analysis of Spanish conveyance and various census records indicates that her plot was on the east bank of Bayou LaFourche approximately eight miles from the Mississippi River.

My research has yet to uncover why Marguerite picked that particular location. The vast majority of the immigrants in this area were Catholic. Since the Spanish had previously established a Catholic church in the area and along with Spanish military post to protect their interest, this may have helped lead to her decision. Perhaps, she simply chose the area because of the other families she knew or was related to decide to settle there.

Figure 9 : Bayou LaFourche Census

Census Year	Total All		Pitre Families			Total Pitres	
	Families	Persons	Ascension	LaFourche	Valenzuela	Families	Persons
1770	84	282				0	
1777	84	485				0	
1788	191	1,075		7		7	27
1791	290	1,191		7		7	21
1795	359	1,775			11	11	20
1797	388	2,064			7	7	22
1798	268	1,693		6		6	13

(Table title within table: Second Acadian Coast — Bayou LaFourche Area)

The LaFourche census of 1788 listed Marguerite Boudrot[(A.b.1741)], widow Pitre, 46 years old, as living on the left bank of Bayou LaFourche. The children listed as residing with her were: Marie [(b.1781; 5-IV)], 25, Madeleine [(b.1763; 5-V)], 23, Olivette [(b.1768; 5-VIII)], 19, Marguerite [(b.1770; 5-IX)], 17, and Jean [(A.b.1780; 5-XIII)], 6. It was noted the family was living on six arpents of land. They also had one swine and 20 quarts of corn. Although Marie [(b.1781;5-IV)], Madeleine [(b.1763;5-V)], and Marguerite [(b.1770;5-IX)] were already married, they were still living on their mother's farm.

1790s

In 1791 the census of LaFourche des Chetimachas recorded on the left bank Anne Pitre, age 50, widow of Gauterau, with her son Jean Pitre, age 11. There might be a possibility that Marguerite Marie Boudrot [(A.b.1741)] had remarried.

The same year census records mention Arman Fremin, age 23, with his wife Marguerite Pitre, age 19, and son Laurent, age 3, had six arpents of land and seven swine.

According to the 1795 census of Valenzuela, Anne Pitre, 55 along with her son Juan [sic "Jean"] Pitre, age 16, were still living at the same location.

The next, 1797 census of Valenzuela in LaFourche Parish also recorded Anne Pitre, widow, 56 and her son Jean, age 17.

I believe with careful analysis these three references identify the same person, Marguerite Marie Boudrot [(A.b.1741)], which many people may have missed because she was recorded as Anne Pitre.

THE 19TH CENTURY

1800s

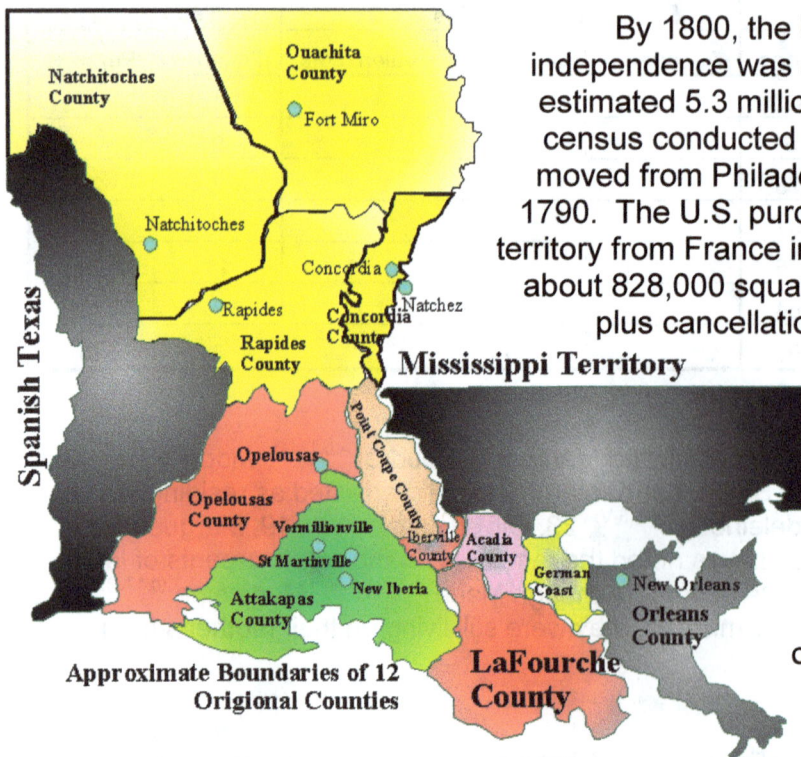

By 1800, the United States of America independence was only 25 years old with an estimated 5.3 million people according to the census conducted in August. The capital was moved from Philadelphia to Washington in 1790. The U.S. purchased the Louisiana territory from France in 1803 which consisted of about 828,000 square miles for $11,250,000 plus cancellation of debts worth about $3.7 million. The price per one acre was around four cents. In June of 1803, President Thomas Jefferson commissioned Meriwether Lewis to explore the Missouri River with hopes of finding a navigable route to the Pacific Ocean.

Map labels: Natchitoches County, Ouachita County, Fort Miro, Natchitoches, Concordia, Natchez, Rapides, Concordia County, Rapides County, Mississippi Territory, Spanish Texas, Opelousas, Point Coupe County, Opelousas County, Vermillionville, Iberville County, Acadia County, St Martinville, New Iberia, German Coast, New Orleans, Orleans County, Attakapas County, LaFourche County, Approximate Boundaries of 12 Origional Counties

In 1803 the Louisiana Territory had come under the jurisdiction of the United States.

On April 10, 1805, the first session of the Legislative Council of the Territory of Orleans passed the Act dividing this territory into twelve counties.

One of them was the "County of Acadia" ("Comte d'Acadie") that connected the parts of the first and second Acadian coasts with lands on both sides of the Mississippi river. The county included church parishes of Ascension and Saint-Jacques.

"County of La Fourche" is another area that presented an interest to my quest since it was the old district and included part of present-day Ascension parish on the west side of Mississippi.

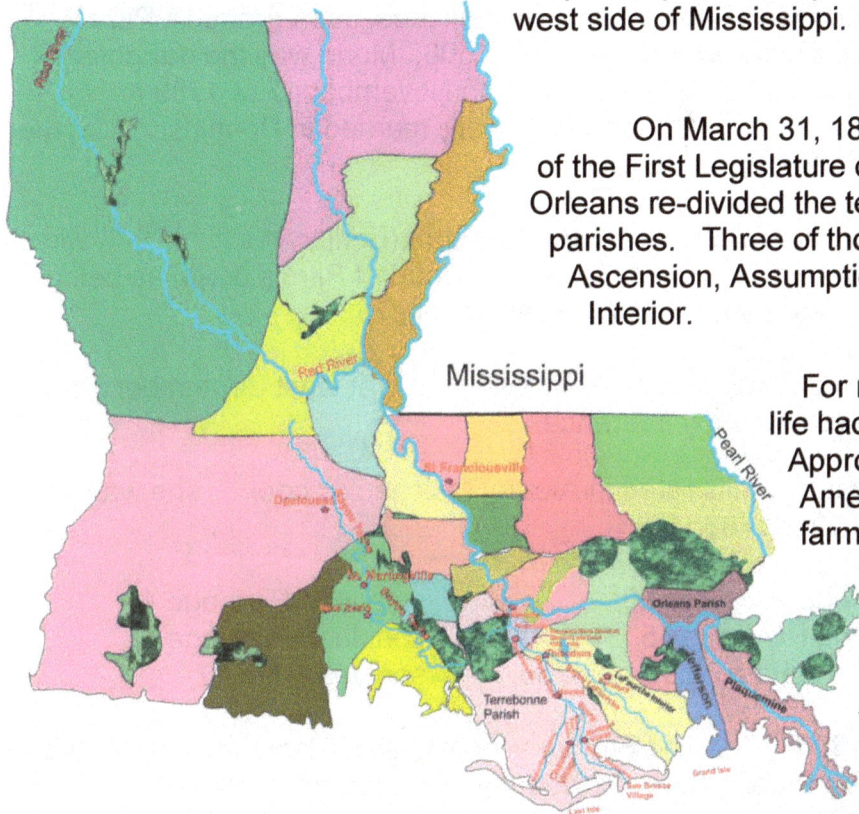

On March 31, 1807, the second session of the First Legislature of the Territory of Orleans re-divided the territory into nineteen parishes. Three of those parishes were Ascension, Assumption, and La Fourche Interior.

For most people, everyday life had changed very little. Approximately 80% of Americans still worked on farms. Average monthly wages in the South ranged from $5 to $9. Farm labor was slightly higher at $10 while non-farm labor was only $1.

Figure 10 : Louisiana Major Waterways mid 1800's

Skilled carpenters were paid $1.50 while those fortunate enough to work in cotton textile industry were getting 50 cents a day. U.S. cotton production was booming with over 200 million pounds per year.

Depending on what part of the country people lived, they could buy a bag of flour for $1.80. Cheap coffee price was 35 cents per pound, while a quarter pound of tea would set you back to 56 cents. A three-and- a-half-pound bag of sugar was sold for $1.05, and if you did not have your own milk cow, you could buy four pounds of butter for $1.60. For those that had a little more money, a milk cow could be bought for around $70, ox for $30, mule for $10, or horse for $25. For two pound of lard one would pay 38 cents, corn meal cost came up to five cents per pound, salt six cents per pound, and beans six cents per pound. To warm up the house, one would spend $1.36 for two bushels of coal. Rent expense added up to $4/week, rifle $15, colt revolver $25, and hunting knife was up to $1.

Now, let us go back to the Pitres and follow their family history throughout the 19th century in Louisiana. As the documentation indicates, Jean Francois Pitre [(A.b.1780; 5-XII)] married Marie Reine Bourg on September 1, 1808. Marie was the daughter of Jean Bourg and Catherine Viaud. She was born on November 17 of 1789 in Donaldsonville, LA. Jean [(A.b.1780; 5-XII)] and Marie were married in Donaldsonville, then settled somewhere along the upper bayou.

It is not known for sure when Marguerite Boudrot (Benjamin's [(A.b.1725; 4-I)] widow) died. All genealogy sites and books list Marguerite Boudrot Pitre's death as being after 1788, because she last appeared in the census of 1788.

However, according to my research, she lived until at least September 1806. The following evidence supports my inference.

According to census details listed in Albert Robichaux's book[15], she was listed in three census records after 1788:

1791	p. 176	Anne Pitre age 50,	son Jean Pitre age 11
1795	p. 60	Ana Pitre age 55,	son Juan Pitre age 16
1797	p. 92	Anne Pitre, widow age 56,	son Jean age 17

On September 24, 1806[16], Armand Fremin acquired some land from his mother-in-law, Marguerite (Boudrot) Pitre. I have not been able to find any recorded transactions indicating how much land or how he acquired it. Therefore, I don't know if he purchased it or inherited it. However, upon closer analysis of factual events in these families timeline yields interesting clues. Out of the six surviving children that stepped off the ship with Marguerite Boudrot Pitre in 1785:

- Marie married Antoine Marin, and they settled near Thibodaux;
- Madeline Modeste died young at the age of 30 in 1793;
- Cecile Olive died before 1800, and there is no any record of her marring;
- Marguerite Charlotte married Armand Philipe Fremin on February 14, 1787 and died on October 3, 1807;
- Etienne died before 1790 with no record of marring;
- Jean married Marie Reine Bourg on September 1, 1808 and decided to settle in Donaldsonville near her parents.

---

[15] Robichaux, Albert, "Colonial Settlers along Bayou Lafourche 1770-1798", Hebert Publications, 1974, pgs 60, 92, 176.

[16] Toups, Kenneth B., Assumption Parish LA Original Cahier Records Books 1 through 5 1786 – 1813, 1991, p75

As I have already mentioned, there is no record of what year Marguerite (Boudrot) Pitre died. However, analyzing the details of Armand Fremin's cash sale on July 12, 1811, the fact that he acquired the land from his mother-in-law, and that his wife, Marguerite Charlotte, passed away in 1807 brings me to a conclusion that Marguerite (Boudrot) Pitre died in 1806. Thus, Marguerite Charlotte (Pitre) and her husband Armand Fremin inherited the land after Marguerite (Boudrot) Pitre's passing.

1810s

In 1810, there was a census conducted along the interior parish of LaFourche. It showed that Jean [(A.b.1780; 5-XII)] and Marie Reine Pitre had decided to settle along the upper Bayou LaFourche near Donaldsonville.

March 31, 1811 came with the birth of Jean [(A.b.1780; 5-XII)] and Marie's first son Jean Florentin Pitre [(A.b.1811; 6-I)], along the banks of Bayou LaFourche in Plattenville, Louisiana. At the age of 29, Jean [(A.b.1780; 5-XII)] was providing for his new family as a farmer along with his wife Marie who was nine years younger.

The second decade of the 19th century might have seemed exciting and changing to some people, but to most hard-working Acadians it was about their daily rigorous labors and efforts to survive. However, when Louisiana was granted statehood on April 30, 1812, politics became one of the prime topics in the various public gathering places, trader outposts along the bayous, shops, and taverns.

The date of Jean Pitre's [((A.b.1780; 5-XII)] death is not known exactly. It is most likely that he died around 1817 in Ascension Parish and was buried near Donaldsonville.

1820s

As of March 22, 1822, with Louisiana being a state, the second session of the Fifth Legislature passed an act establishing the "Parish of Terre Bonne" out of the Parish of LaFourche Interior.

1830s

In 1832, Jean Florentin Pitre [(A.b.1811; 6-I)] married his first wife. Marie Modeste Azélie Thibodeaux was born in Plattenville on January 31, 1812 down Bayou LaFourche near Plattenville. They were married on July 23, 1832 in Thibodaux. Marie was the daughter of Jean Baptiste Thibodeaux and Martine Hache. Jean Florentin Pitre [(A.b.1811; 6-I)] and Marie had three children, all born in Thibodaux. Florentin Marcel Pitre was born on January 16, 1834, Jean Aurélien Pitre was born in February, 1837, and Marcellite Elise Pitre was born in October, 1838. Marie was only

27 years old when she died around 1839. During that time they lived near Thibodeaux, Louisiana. Therefore, Marie is most likely buried in Thibodeaux.

Later that year, in 1832 Jean Florentin Pitre's [(A.b.1811; 6-I)] mother, Marie Reine (Bourg) Pitre died on November 10. She was also living near Thibodaux at the time. She was Jean Francois Pitre's [(A.b.1780; 5-XII)] wife. She was most likely buried in Thibodaux as well.

1840s

On August 31 of 1840, Jean Florentin Pitre [(A.b.1811; 6-I)] married his second wife Susanne Zulmie Toups. The ceremony took place at St. Joseph Church in Thibodaux. Susanne was born on October 8, 1816 down Bayou LaFourche near Plattenville.   Her parents were Drauzin Joseph Toups and Judith Mayer. Drauzin was a German Creole from Des Allemands Louisiana. Judith was also from Des Allemands.

Jean Florentin Pitre [(A.b.1811; 6-I)] must have moved from lower Bayou LaFourche south of Plattenville to Thibodaux area sometime between 1840 and 1841 because Élie Pierre Pitre [(A.b.1841; 7-IV)] was born in Thibodaux. By the end of 1940s, Jean Florentin Pitre [(A.b.1811; 6-I)] had four children with Susanne, all of which were born in Thibodaux Louisiana. Élie Pierre [(A.b.1841; 7-IV)] born on August 26, 1841, Joseph Aiser [(b.1843; 7-V)] born on March 28, 1843, Louis Jean Olesime [(b.1845; 7-VI)] born on April 5, 1845. Pierre William [(b.1848; 7-VII)] born on June 2, 1848.   Élie Pierre Pitre [(A.b.1811; 7-IV)] is my great-great-grandfather, pronounced [Alie].

1850s

In 1850, Florentin Pitre [(A.b.1811; 6-I)] (as he was called then) and his family were listed as living in Jefferson City during the Barataria census[17]. Jefferson City was a census-designated place in Jefferson Parish on the east bank of the Mississippi River. It is now part of Metairie, Kenner, and New Orleans, LA. Therefore, Jean Florentin Pitre [(A.b.1811; 6-I)] probably moved from Thibodaux to Barataria sometime between 1841 and 1850. It is not clear how he provided for his family at this time since all that was documented indicates his occupations as a "laborer". However, there were several large plantations in this area. Most likely, he was a field plow hand. At the age of 38 years old, he moved from Assumption Parish to Jefferson Parish, but there is no documentation providing the reasons for his relocation. We can only assume the move happened in search of the better opportunities for his growing family near New

---

[17] Ancestry.com. *1850 United States Federal Census* [database on-line]. Provo, UT, USA: Ancestry.com Operations, Inc., 2009. Images reproduced by FamilySearch. Index: Louisiana, Jefferson, Barataria, Image 14 of 16, line 16.

Orleans. Along with his wife Susanne, who was 30 years old at that time, they had five children living with them: Marcellite [(b.1838; 7-III)], 14, Élie [(A.b.1841; 7-IV)], 9, Isaac [(b.1843; 7-V)], 7, Olesie [(b.1845; 7-VI)], 6, and William [(b.1848; 7-VIII)], 2.

Jefferson City, originally a part of Jefferson Parish, was incorporated as Jefferson City in 1850. By 1860, its population was 5,107. It was annexed by the City of New Orleans in 1870. The Louisiana Department of Culture, Recreation and Tourism placed the marker in 1979. There is a historical marker located in a neighborhood near a commercial stretch of Magazine Street.

Sometime in the late 1850s, Élie Pierre Pitre [(A.b.1841; 7-IV)] decided he did not want to be a farmer like his father and grandfather. Since he was living in Jefferson City, which was very close to New Orleans, he often heard stories of the adventurers who lived as trappers and coastal anglers along the gulf. Being enticed by an opportunity to begin a new life, he decided to take on an adventure on the coast. Thus, he settled on the northeastern end of what some people referred to as Grand Chénière. After extensive research, I found only two sources to help authenticate the plausibility of this—Wisteria's documented interviews (Wisteria's oral recordings, transcription of 2013) and Élie Pitre's property records in Terrebonne parish[18]. Unfortunately, Élie Pitre [(A.b.1841; 7-IV)] did not appear anywhere in the 1860 census. An important note, he was also not listed as living with his parents during the 1860 census. That makes it possible to imply that he had previously moved away. A few other Pitre families had previously moved away from Platteville to Grand Chénière just before 1950. Some of these families can be directly traced as descendants of Claude Jean Pitre [(b.1727; 3-II)] or third cousins of Élie Pitre [(A.b.1841; 7-IV)]. Claude Jean Pitre [(b.1727; 3-II)] and Benjamin Pitre [(A.b.1725; 3-I)] were brothers, both born in Corbequit, Acadia.

Chénière Caminada is also widely known to locals as Grand Chénière at the time. Chénière was a local French and creole word meaning "oak ridge". Thus, Grand Chénière means "large oak ridge." Chénière Caminada was the last inland finger just before reaching Grand Isle. The chain of Chénière had an elevation of several feet above sea level. Unlike the barrier islands, the Chénières had plenty of underground fresh water, which allowed oak trees to thrive. In the 1830s, the landowners on Grand Isle developed their land as cotton and sugar cane plantations. However, Caminadaville remained dependent on hunting and fishing. With tourists who came to the coast for surf bathing along with the oyster, fish, and turtle trade, it was easy for locals to make a decent living there.

---

[18] Westerman, Audrey. Memorial to Chénière Caminada "E. P. Pitre" line 14, page 31

There is no official record of Élie Pitre's [(A.b.1841; 7-IV)] first marriage. However, his first wife's maiden name was Jambon. According to my research, I estimate they married young, sometime around 1856 and 1858. Approximately around 1859, she was pregnant with their first child. Unfortunately, with a fever of 107, she died of yellow fever. They had been married only for two years. Élie could not even leave his yard to bury her due to yellow flags placed everywhere marking the yellow fever quarantine. So he had little to no choice and decided to dismantle part of his chicken coup to make a coffin and burry her in his back yard. When he told that story, he said it was one of the most difficult things he ever had to do (from Élie Pitre's granddaughter Wisteria's oral recordings, transcription of 2013). That area has long washed away because of erosion and storms. The Federal Government imposed mandatory quarantines up and down the Mississippi delta as well as other areas in the US. The quarantines in and around Orleans and Jefferson parishes lasted from 1820s through 1855 with pockets springing up through 1860. Over 41,000 people died from the disease around New Orleans between 1817 and 1905, 1850s seeming to be the peak[19]. Élie [(A.b.1841; 7-IV)] would sometimes boast that he never caught fellow fever.

1860s

At the age of 49 years old, Florentin Pitre [(A.b.1811; 6-I)] was still living somewhere around Jefferson City. He was working as a field laborer on one of the plantations along the mighty Mississippi.

I do not know exactly the year when the following story took place; nevertheless, after extensive research and analysis, I came to a conclusion that it could only have been either 1853 or 1860. Currently, I am leaning toward 1860. Let us get to the story though. During the fall, some local women came by to invite Élie [(A.b.1841; 7-IV)] to go with them to the dance hall. He decided to decline the invitation because he knew there was really bad weather coming. Élie [(A.b.1841; 7-IV)] and his friend (possibly a brother) decided to ride out the storm in their boat. When they saw a break in the storm, they climbed up the biggest tree they could find. They were able to survive the storm by tying themselves to the tree. A third wave hit the ridge and completely wiped out the dance hall—all who were there were gone. According to Élie's [(A.b.1841; 7-IV)] telling of the events, his friend and he were the only two survivors on Grand Chénière.

On April 12, 1861, Confederate forces fired upon Fort Sumter; it was the beginning of the Civil War in the United States. With escalating hostilities, Florentin Pitre [(A.b.1811; 6-I)] decided he did not want death and destruction to touch his family.

---

[19] --- http://nutrias.org/facts/feverdeaths.htm ---

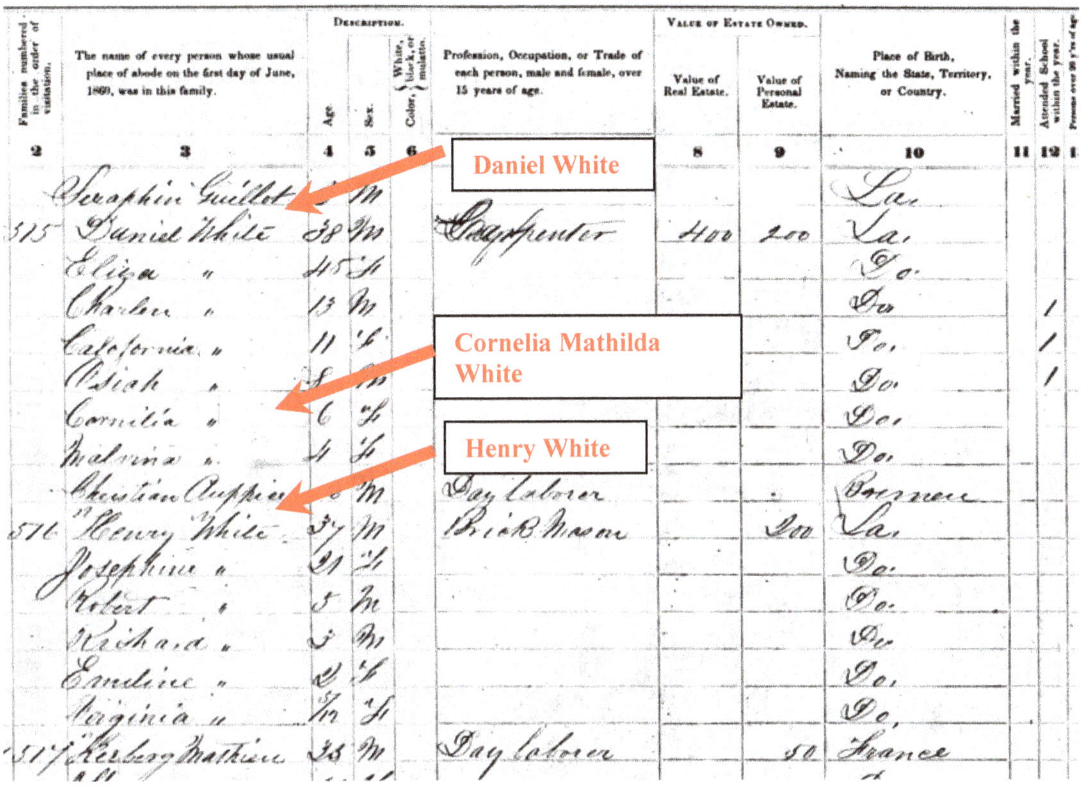

Figure 11 : 1860 US Federal Census, Terrebonne Parish, 8th Ward, Page # 73

Therefore, he chose to move his family away from New Orleans and the coast. They settled near the small community of Raceland where they thought they were far enough from the main ports and waterways. After losing everything in hurricane, in addition to the death of his wife from yellow fever, Élie [(A.b.1841; 7-IV)] also decided to move away from the coast and join his parents near Raceland.

The 1860 census recorded details about Daniel White's family[20]. During the upcoming 1870s, he would become my third great grandfather, Cornelia Mathilda White's farther. During this time, Daniel was a 48 year old carpenter living on the Right bank of Bayou LaFourche in the northern edge of Terrebonne Parish. For more details on Daniel White, refer to the last page of the "My Family Tree" appendix.

Some publications stated that Hubert Madison Belanger dug Madison Canal in 1870 by hand with a spade. Initially, it was only wide enough for his pirogue. However, he died on March 28, 1855. Therefore, he had to complete digging the canal sometime before 1850. Boudreaux Canal was also built in 1850 and Bush Canal around 1890.

[20] Ancestry.com. *1860 United States Federal Census* [database on-line]. Provo, UT, USA: Ancestry.com Operations, Inc., 2009. Images reproduced by FamilySearch. Index: 1860, Louisiana, Terrebonne, Ward 8, Image 14.

Sometime just after 1800, a surveyor by the name of Thomas Rhodes came into lower Terrebonne Parish. He settled just below present day Bush Canal. On September 4, 1860 Thomas Rhodes, Jr. (b.03/21/1838 Thibodaux) married Victoria Dometille (Use) (b.12/17/1841 Thibodaux in Houma) and settled in Ward 6 near Bush Canal along lower Bayou Terrebonne. Thomas was a boat builder, farmer, and oyster fisherman. He and three family members were buried on top of the old Indian mound. In the mid-1870s, my second great grandparents would settle down 9 homesteads up Bayou LaCache from Thomas and Victoria. The other Thomas's son was Robert, who owned a large dance hall at Bush Canal. Although, there were several dance halls along lower Bayou Terrebonne, it seems that one was the closest to my second great-grandparents homestead. Further in this book, I will tell a story that explains how the abovementioned information played a significant part in my first great-grandparents meeting.

While attending to his duties along lower Bayou Terrebonne, Father Denece noticed that the road going through the Collein property needed some improvements. Therefore, in 1866, he spent $15 to build a bridge across Bayou LaCache. Two years later, he was able to raise enough donations to improve the road running between the two bayous. Bayou LaCache became named according to the story of finding some of Jean Lafitte's treasure, which refers to "something hidden or to hide".

1870s

Around 1875, Lee Yim, a Chinese businessman, left his home in Canton, China, and immigrated to Terrebonne Parish, LA. There he used knowledge he acquired from his native home and founded a very successful shrimp drying business.

Figure 12 : Shrimp Drying Platform, Lower Terrebonne

The census of 1870 further documented Jean Florentin Pitre (A.b.1811; 6-I) relocating from Barataria to Raceland. Florentin Pete (A.b.1811; 6-I) [sic] was listed as a 59 year-old field laborer with his wife Susanne (A.b.1816), 54, a house keeper, and their children: Alea [Élie] (A.b.1841; 7-IV), 30, field laborer, Marie (b.1859), 14, assisting father, Drosane (b.1860), 7 (Raceland, W3, p. 62).

While living with his parents near Raceland, Élie Pierre Pitre [(A.b.1841; 7-IV)] traveled down the bayous selling fruit with an Italian friend, whose name was Pascal. I could not find out his last name. On one of such trips, Élie [(A.b.1841; 7-IV)] stopped at Henry White's homestead on the right bank along Bayou LaFourche and asked for a place to sleep. Élie [(A.b.1841; 7-IV)] was told he could sleep in the yard with Henry's sons. During that time, this was the custom practice. Boys of age were not allowed to sleep inside the house when young girls were there. While there, Élie [(A.b.1841; 7-IV)] met Mathilda Cornelia White living wither her uncle. Élie said she was the most beautiful girl he ever met. According to him, she was six feet tall and had long blond hair. According to her Baptismal records, Cornelia was born in Terrebonne Parish on October 7, 1853. She was baptized by Reverend FS Tasset on September 25, 1854 at St Francis De Sales in Houma.

When it was time to leave, Élie [(A.b.1841; 7-IV)] told Henry that he was falling in love with his beautiful niece and asked permission to marry her. Élie [(A.b.1841; 7-IV)] also explained his own position sharing the story about his first wife who died of yellow fever. Henry responded that Cornelia was already engaged to be married to someone else.

Cornelia was going to marry Lash Hendigriff. On the morning of the wedding, they butchered a hog and had five barrels of oysters for the reception. However, Hendigriff never showed up. Later the Whites found out that he was engaged to two different girls. He decided to marry the other one. After that accident, Henry gave Élie [(A.b.1841; 7-IV)] permission to marry Cornelia but insisted the ceremony to be conducted in the Catholic Church down in Montegut. I have not found any official records to verify they were married in Sacred Heart Church south of Montegut. Especially, since Henry White's homestead was right next door to his brother's former homestead along Bayou LaFourche. In 1819, Saint Joseph church was built along the banks of Bayou LaFourche, near the present day Catholic cemetery.

As it was agreed, on September 13, 1873, Élie Pierre Pitre [(A.b.1841; 7-IV)] married Cornelia Mathilda White in the Sacred Heart Church just south of the village of Montegut. The original church no longer exists. Initially the church was where Dugas Cemetery is located today. The property was originally donated to the community by Jean Baptiste Dugas, known by many as "The Hermit of Montegut"[21]. The construction of the church started in August of 1867 and completed by 1870 under the direction of Father Jean Marie Joseph Denece, pastor of Houma. This was actually the second Catholic Church built for the congregation since they had outgrown the first building.

---

[21] "Hermit of Montegut" Guidry, Sherwin. Le Terrebonne – A History of Montegut

Researching old records about Cornelia White, I detected that Cornelia's legal last name prior to marring Élie Pierre Pitre [(A.b.1841; 7-IV)] was Price. This is because her mother's legal name was Eliza Price. At the time Cornelia was born, Eliza was not married to Daniel White as previously mentioned. Therefore, one should use both Price and White when looking for official records regarding Cornelia, such as census logs, Church records, ship passenger lists, etc.

Henry White, Cornelia's uncle with whom she was living at that time, died before 1880 census.

Figure 13 : Lower Bayou Terrebonne, Circa 1900

Having more adventurous blood than his parents did, Élie [(A.b.1841; 7-IV)] decided he could not stay away from the coast. He wanted more in life for his new family. Thus, he carved out a new homestead on lower Bayou Terrebonne, about five homesteads down from Cornelia's parents. After all, the bustling community of Sea Breeze was only eight miles south of the Bayou LaCache community. At the time, it seemed well protected from the devastation of hurricanes he previously experienced in Barataria. Bayou Terrebonne was once an outlet of the Mississippi River via Bayou LaFourche, but due to a closure at Bayou LaFourche in the years prior to 1880, the upper bayou silted in and navigation above Houma became impossible.

There, at Bayou LaCache, about eight miles south of Montegut, Élie [(A.b.1841; 7-IV)] built a house for his new wife, Cornelia. The property bordered Bayou Terrebonne in the east and Bayou LaCache in the west. In those days, when a person acquired property along one of the bayous of south Terrebonne parish, that property usually stretched between the bayous. As common for that time and location, Élie built the house using roughly squared cypress trees and mud for insulation. Palmetto leaves were used for roof and walls. For the floor, he used compacted clay that was easily found along the bayous.

Figure 14 : Common Hut made of Palmetto & Cypress, Lower Bayou Terrebonne, circa 1860

According to Cornelia's first-born grandchild, Wisteria Pitre [(b.1898; 9-I)], her grandmother was from Honduras and came to the United States with her parents when she was very young. However, according to the official records of Diocese of Houma-Thibodaux, Cornelia was born and baptized in Houma. Cornelia was in Central America in 1869 according to Steamer Trade Wind ship logs of arriving passengers[22].

Cornelia White was of English decent. She spoke very little French and, according to other surviving grandchildren, Cornelia did not speak Spanish. Cornelia was born in Houma, Louisiana. The 1860 census lists her living with her parents at the age of 6 near Bayou LaFourche in Terrebonne. One surviving document of interest lists Cornelia Price as coming back from Belize to New Orleans with her mother Eliza Price. There is no record of Eliza Price marring Daniel White. In 1860, Eliza's first husband, John Price, was still living. That along with the official last names on the ship log supports that theory. Daniel's brother, Henry White, a 38-year-old mechanic also accompanied them. The purpose of their trip is unknown at this time. Perhaps after Daniel White died, they all went down to South America along with Henry White while he worked on temporary mechanic jobs there. I also think that

---

[22] National Archives Microfilm, Microcopy 259 Roll 53, Image 0306 and 0307

Daniel White had already died sometime between the 1860 census and 1868. Therefore, with this added information, I do not believe that Élie [A.b.1841; 7-IV] ever met Daniel White. Besides, it was at Daniel's brother's house where he first met Cornelia.

Most references I found that listed a date and place claim that she was born on October 7, 1850 in Houma, Louisiana. According to her age on US Census documents, she would have been born in 1854. However, the date of birth listed on her death certificate was October 12, 1852. I would like to add one more important fact to help settle the mystery of her birth year. According to her Baptismal records from the Diocese of Houma-Thibodeaux, she was born on October 7, 1853 and baptized on September 25, 1954.

According to Cornelia's obituary, she was 82, making her birth year to be 1852. The obituary account was based on what Cornelia (White) Pitre told her children and grandchildren at different times. There is no known documented record of her birth, and it is likely that Cornelia did not know for sure herself what year she was born. Based on my analysis of all the data I have reviewed, 1852 seems to be more plausible in reference with other events.

The census records also state that all of Daniel's children were born in Louisiana. Perhaps, Wisteria misunderstood her grandmother or did not remember details correctly. Based on my analysis of historical timelines, I believe Cornelia was born in Louisiana.

Analyzing discrepancies in some facts and dates as told by Wisteria, I am inclined to think that it is possible that Wisteria [b.1898; 9-I] could confuse events and dates with that of various relatives because she told those stories later in life and could simply forget some details. It is more likely that her husband's ancestors came from Central America unlike Cornelia's family.

Concerning Cornelia's parents, there are very few documents and census information. I have not established solid evidence where and when Daniel White was born. However, it is worth noting that Daniel's second wife Eliza Pierce was born in 1815 in Iberville parish. It is believed they were married in 1846 in Louisiana.

As to the issue of whether or not Daniel White previously changed his name from Daniel Nettleton, there is not any known documentation proving that name change had happened.

In the 1850 census a Daniel Nettleton is listed along Bayou LaFourche as being 48 years old. In 1860 census, is a 38-year-old carpenter, listed as living in the same area. Also, the children names are different in both censuses. There is a land purchase document dated June 13, 1844, with Daniel Nettleton's name listed as the purchaser. It describes purchase of 49.8 acres of land in the township of LaFourche parish. I did not find any reference to a Daniel White or Nettleton of the appropriate age in the 1870 census and onwards. Without further hard government or church records, I feel that Daniel Nettleton and Daniel White were two different men living in the same area during the middle 1800's. A careful study of each of the 1850 and 1860 census clearly reviles multiple people by the same name. Cornelia also claimed that her parents were of English decent.

According to my research, Eliza (Pierce) White's parents were Daniel L. Pierce born 1787 in Westmoreland and Mary Elizabeth Sons born 1795 in New Hampshire. Wisteria also stated that her grandmother said that Daniel and Mary Pierce were also of English decent.

Eliza Pierce's first husband, John Price, was still living during the 1860 census. Also, no record of Eliza and Daniel's marriage have been found. Therefore, its speculated they may have been co-habituating even though they had several children together[23].

Eliza and John Price's last child was born on January 3, 1846, its presumed they separated shortly after that. Also, Daniel White and Eliza Price's first child, was born in 1847. Thus indicating that John and Eliza Price separated in 1846. There is no record of John and Eliza getting a divorce. In addition there is no official record of Daniel and Eliza getting married. There are however, official records listing Eliza's last name as Price several years after she was living with Daniel. I'll leave it up to the readers to do their own research and make up their own conclusions, but the facts speak for them self on what seems to have happened. For more detailed information about Daniel and Eliza's family, refer to the last page of the "My Family Tree" appendix in this book.

23 Eliza Pierce http://wc.rootsweb.ancestry.com/cgi-bin/igm.cgi?op=GET&db=cynthiadaigle&id=I029175

By the end of the 1870s, Élie[(A.b.1841; 7-IV)] and Cornelia had three children, all born somewhere along lower Bayou Terrebonne, within the 14 miles radius south of Montegut: Jemmy Joseph Pitre [(b.1874; 8-I)] born on June 17, 1874, John Lee Pitre [(A.b.1876; 8-II)] born on June 2, 1876, Lenius Élie Pitre [(b.1878; 8-III)] born on May 1, 1878. John Lee Pitre [(A.b.1876; 8-II)] is my great-grandfather and was baptized on September 29, 1876 by Reverend J.M. J. Denece at Sacred Heart Church.

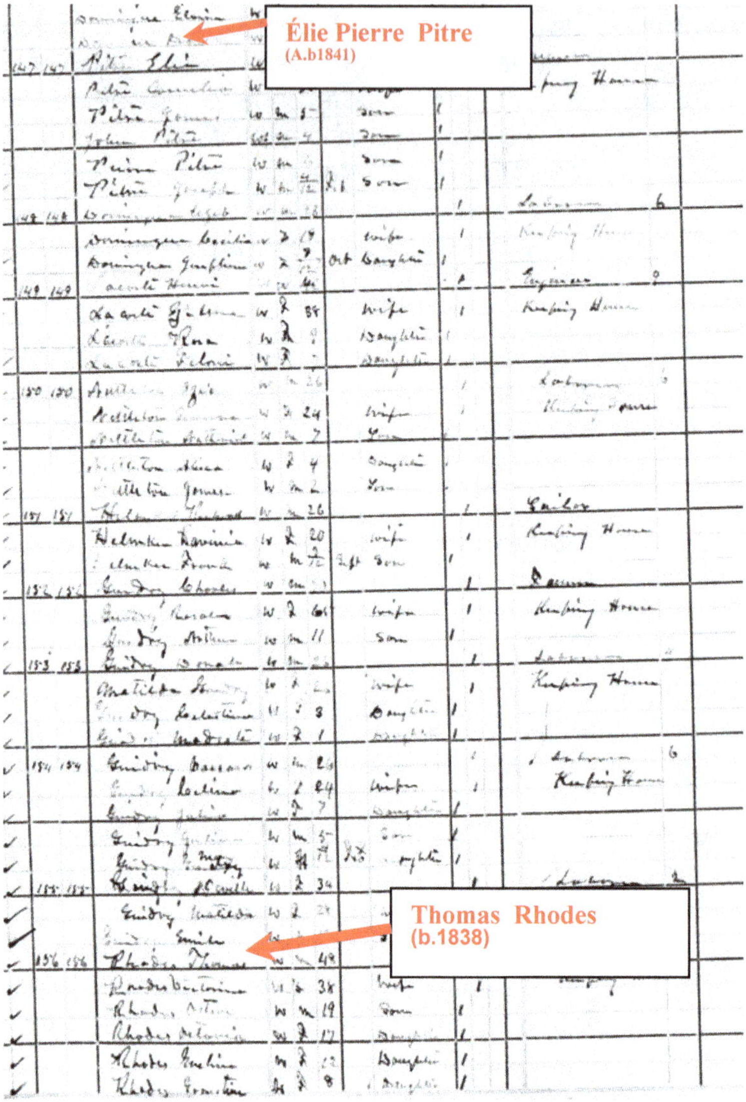

1880s

During the turn of the 1880s, travel to Grand Isle from New Orleans in 8 hours by steamer for $2.

In 1889, the village of Montegut was named after one of its most distinguished residents, Colonel Gabriel Montegut.

Figure 15 : 1880 US Federal Cencus recording of Pitre & Rhodes

The 1880's census documented my third great-grandparents as living near Raceland in Lafourche Parish. A 69 year-old farmer at the time, Jean Florentin Pitre [(A.b.1811; 6-I)] was living in district 132 of ward 6. His 64 year-old second wife Susanne Zulmie (Toups) was also recorded along with their daughter Marie (b.1859), 24, and son Drauzin (b.1860), 19 working as a laborer.

Meanwhile, the Terrebonne Census[24], in district 190 of ward 6, listed a 35 year-old Élie Pitre [(A.b.1841; 7-IV)] working as a farmer, along with his wife Amelia (this is how

[24] Year: *1880*; Census Place: *6th Ward, Terrebonne, Louisiana*; Roll: *472*; Family History Film: *1254472*; Page: *316B*; Enumeration District: *190*; Image: *0637*

Cornelia was spelled), 30, as house wife. Their homestead was on the banks of Bayou Terrebonne inside the Sixth Ward of Terrebonne Parish, near present day Montegut. Not sure what this means, but the census listed Élie [A.b.1841; 7-IV] as 12 homesteads after Josephine White's (Henry White's widow) house. The distance between Bayou LaFourche and Montegut on Bayou Terrebonne is rather significant. By this time they had four children living: Jemmy Joseph[b.1874;8-I], 5, John Lee[A.b:1876; 8-II], 1876, 4, Lennuis Élie [b.1878; 8-III], 2, Richard Peter[b.1880; 8-IV], 4 months.

Jean Florentin Pitre [A.b.1811; 6-I] died on the 27 of October, 1886, near Thibodaux, Louisiana. Due to the absence of further documentation, we can only guess that Susanne Toups died sometime after 1880.

Élie [A.b.1841; 7-IV] and Cornelia's first born child, Jemmy Joseph Pitre[b.1874; 8-I] died on November 20 of 1886. He contracted blood poisoning after bitten by a black widow spider.

1890s

Unfortunately, there are very few records left from the 1980 US Federal census. Most of the documents were destroyed by fire on January 10, 1921. However, fortunately, numerous details of the time survived through many other sources.

Life along lower Bayou Terrebonne was thriving. Pretty much anything a southern bayou family needed was there. They even had a General Store owned by Gabriel Bourg, Leon "Crick" Rhodes' Store, and Louis Polencot Dance Hall just above Bush canal. Also, Robert Rhodes, constable, owned a large dance hall at Bush Canal.

Many details of John Lee Pitre's [A.b.1876; 8-II] childhood may have been lost to history. He had a striking blond hair, blue eyes, and a short stature. Like most Pitre men, he was of a proud, yet humble origin living on the land just like his ancestors before him. I do not know what type of work John [A.b.1874 8-II] did during his early teen years, but it was probably trapping and oyster fishing with his father. He never attended school and could not read or write. Therefore, like all young men of the time, it is most likely that he started working at a very early age doing whatever he could find. The only jobs available along lower Bayou Terrebonne were farm laborer, trapping muskrat for furs, oyster fishing and shrimping, unless someone was fortunate to land a job with Texaco. A little further north, some lucky few could find jobs as an oyster shucker or oyster canning factory. During that time, oysters were selling in lower Terrebonne for 60 cents a bushel.

In 1891 Charles Benjamin Maginnis and Reuben G. Bush, Sr. founded the Lower Terrebonne Refining and Manufacturing Company and built a sugar refinery in Montegut. Charles was married to Reuben's sister, Susan Kar Bush. They had also planted sugar cane along Bayou Petit Caillou. Soon after, Reuben acquired the right away from the family of Thomas Rhodes and dug a narrow canal connecting the two bayous, so that he could more easily transport his cane from Bayou Petit Caillou over to the refinery on Bayou Terrebonne. Reuben died on February 3, 1912 while at his son's house in New Orleans.

There were many bars and houses with makeshift dance halls along the bayou. Cornelia (White) Pitre would make some money cleaning the floors of some of those dancing halls after their closing for the night. During that time, Cornelia befriended Lucie Marie (Vitto) Autin. Lucie was partly of Italian descent, married to Charles Autin. Cornelia quickly gained Lucie's confidence and trust. Lucie explained to Cornelia that when her husband, Charles, was not working he was home and usually drunk. He was very abusive to their daughter Francis and forced her to work in the fields from a very young age. Francis had few clothes and no shoes.

One day around 1893, when Lucie was talking to Cornelia, she decided it was too dangerous for Francis to stay around her father. Lucie knew that Cornelia had daughters of her own and had a very good reputation of raising them properly. So she asked Cornelia if she would take Francis in her place and finish raising her. Cornelia promised Lucie she would do her best and explained that her boys always slept outside in the boats and did not bother girls. From then on, Francis slept inside with her daughters.

Francis was about 4'10" tall with dark hair. She was born on March 29, 1879 and baptized on May 27 by Reverend J. M. J. Denece at Sacred Heart Church. At the time, she could speak only Cajun French and did not understand English. As soon as Francis moved in, Cornelia's three sons got together and pooled the little money they had to buy Francis her first pair of shoes.

One night in 1895, John [A.b.1876; 8-II], 19 years old at the time, told his mom that it was two years that he had been dating Francis. He said he loved her and wanted to get married. Francis was now 16. They realized there was no reason in asking Francis's father since he was always drunk and did not care much about anyone. However, Cornelia said even though Lucie gave her permission to make all decisions regarding Francis, they needed to go and ask Lucie. So John and one of his sisters went to Lucie to ask her permission. John promised his future mother-in-law that he would take very good care of Francis and they would live with his mother until he was able to provide a home of their own.

On May 5, 1896 John and Francis were married by Father Corneliar, a French priest, in Houma. During that time, John's [(A.b.1876; 8-II)] primary occupation was oyster fishing. He decided to settle his new family along lower Bayou LaCache a few homesteads from his parents, just south of Bush canal; it was about nine miles below Montegut. His land track was bordered on the west by bayou Petit Caillou and on the east by Bayou LaCache. Having no money, John carved out a place along the bayou and built a hut out of palmetto.

Palmetto-covered bousillage homes were built by Houma Indians and were a common sight along the bayous of Terrebonne parish. With the ground as a floor, they lined it with cured moss and cornhusks or whatever else they could find. Some accounts state people used to cook in a fireplace, but it is unknown if fire places were made of stone or bricks. Since they had little to no money, most likely it was a clay fireplace or maybe even discarded bricks they picked up.

Towards the end of the 19th century, John Pitre [(A.b.1876; 8-II)] found himself living along the marshy bayou as a hardworking man humbly occupied with whatever the land could provide. During that time, John [(A.b.1876; 8-II)] was an oyster fisherman.

The winter of 1896 was unusually cold in the marshlands of south Louisiana. As if life was not hard enough along the bayous, the residents along lower Terrebonne Bayou found themselves having to survive with as much as three feet of snow on the ground. One has to remember the average house along lower Bayou Terrebonne was of simple construction made mostly of mud, palmetto leaves between roughly squared cypress boards.

On a very cold day of January 3, a snowy winter day in 1897 John [(A.b.1876; 8-II)] and Francis just became proud parents with the birth of their first child. Their daughter was born premature and weighted two pounds and two ounces due to her mother having measles at the time. Although the nearest hospital was over 20 miles away in Houma, a few doctors lived along the bayous.

At first the newborn's Uncle Ellis [(b.1885)] and John [(A.b.1876; 8-II)] thought the baby-girl was dead. However, realizing she was alive, they wrapped her in cotton and olive oil. Then they placed her in a cigar box to use as a makeshift baby bed. They would later boast about being able to put Francis's wedding ring around the baby's arm. She was named by her grandfather Élie Pierre Pitre[(A. b. 1840; 7-IV)] after a popular local wine made from an edible wild flower known as Wisteria[(b.1897; 9-I)] (also spelled Wysteria). She was given her Christian name of Maria during her baptism soon after the birth.

When Wisteria [(b1897; 9-I)] was born, her parents had little comforts. Their home was as simple and modest as could be found along the lower bayous. The mud and palmetto lined cypress house John built had a dirt floor. It was not uncommon to pound clay from the riverbank into the ground to use as a makeshift floor inside their huts. They did not have any cows, but John did own a few goats. So they would often feed goat milk to the kids after their mother stopped nursing them when they reached an age of two and a half years.

On February 8 of 1898, John and Francis Pitre [A.b.1876 8-II] gave birth to their second child, Élie Pitre [A.b1898; 9-II]. Élie [A.b1898; 9-II] (pronounced [Alie]) is my paternal grandfather. During his baptism on April 29, 1899, they named him Joseph. He was baptized by Reverend C. Richard at Sacred Heart Church.

By the end of the 1890s, Élie Pierre Pitre [A.b. 1841; 7-IV] and Cornelia had nine children together. Since all of them were born somewhere along lower Terrebonne Bayou below Montegut, they were still living along the Bayou LaCache.

Élie Pierre Pitre [A.b. 1841; 7-IV] died of inflammatory rheumatism on April 19, 1898 in his home along lower Bayou Terrebonne. People did not understand rheumatism, its symptoms, and treatments very well in those times; even the doctors had missed correct diagnosis. In many cases, death was a result of misdiagnosis or simply due to complications of poorly understood and treated disease.

THE 20TH CENTURY

1900s

At the onset of the 1900s, life was somewhat more prosperous and self-fulfilling for the people of south Louisiana.

Figure 16 : Central Terrebonne 1900

The lush cypress and oak forests and waterways provided everything they needed to thrive. Most that did not find regular jobs working for the farms, refineries, or seafood processing plants were trappers, shrimpers, or oyster fishermen. Some were fortunate to sign on with Texaco drilling operations in the marsh.

From the cane refineries, shrimp drying platforms, and the oyster canners, everyone was benefiting from the rapid growth.

The Sea Breeze community down lower Bayou Terrebonne was at its peak at the 20th century rolled in.

According to US census data, the 20th century came roaring in with about 76 million people living in the United States[25]. Among them only about 3% of homes had electricity and less than a third had running water. Most people worked within a mile of where they lived. As much as 10% of the population was completely illiterate.

Nationwide food prices were rather low for those that had paying jobs. You could get five pounds of flour for 12 cents, bread for five cents per loaf, a pound of bacon went for 14 cents, and butter cost 26 cents per pound. A dozen of fresh eggs were sold for 20cents, and a gallon of milk was 27cents.

---

[25] http://www.census.gov/history/www/through_the_decades/

In contrast, good paying jobs were not so easy to find along the Louisiana bayous in the Deep South. However, in those days the families did not have a lack of wild seafood and wild game. If people were willing to hunt, the nature was generous with its resources.

Wild ducks were plentiful, and hunters did not have any seasonal or quantity limits at that time. Sometimes, the marsh was completely covered with ducks for hundreds of square miles. It was common for the hunters to eat boney parts while at their camps or on their fishing boats. After that, they would pack the precooked meaty parts in kegs with lard to bring back home for summer.

Along the brackish bayous, crabs were more copious than one can imagine today. They would swim right up to the edge of the banks, and the only thing to do was to scoop them up, literally. These same bayous were also overflowing with shrimp and fish. In addition, Louisiana marsh was brimming with muskrats, minks, and otters, and the trappers took full advantage of those.

Some families raised hogs, which they would kill in the fall and save lard for other uses. Many would take salt pork and lard to their winter camps along the marsh.

Although the shrimping industry was building up due to the success and popularity of the drying process, oysters were still predominant among most fishermen. The Cajuns would use small wind powered sail boats to dredge for oysters. Boats sailed from oyster reefs on coast up Bayou Terrebonne until they got to Bush Canal, then cross over to Bayou Petit Caillou into Chauvin. From Chauvin they would pay $2.50 to be transported up to Houma.

Houma was considered the oyster canning capital of the world. Chauvin Brothers also had a large oyster processing facility in Chauvin. Oysters were shucked there prior to being shipped to Houma. A sack of oysters in the shell was usually sold for 25 cents and could go up to 50 cents. Shuckers were paid 75 cents per thousand oysters. Shucked oysters sold between 75 cents to $1 per barrel. The facility in Houma would process between 40 and 50 thousand barrels of steamed oysters per year.

One of my great-grandfather's younger brothers, Lenius Élie Pitre [b.1878; 8-III], known as Uncle Lee, was a hardworking oyster fisherman. He would try to get 5 cents for a bushel of oysters from the locals, but very few people living along bayou Terrebonne at the time had cash money. He often traveled to New Orleans where he could sell for higher prices. However, the journey was long and hard. It would usually take about two weeks one way up Bayou Terrebonne through Houma via Bayou

Caine until he eventually reached Bayou LaFourche. In those days, Bayou LaFourche was connected to the Mississippi River.

The shrimping industry was certainly thriving with the new drying process started by the Chinese immigrants. Several large shrimp drying platforms popped up along the coast near Sea Breeze, as well as along the marsh areas around Grand Isle. The majority of the drying platforms were originated and owned by the Chinese. Most shrimp and fish were dried raw in the sun after curing in brine. Fresh fish was gutted and placed in brine barrel for few days till cured and then hung to dry. Cured fish was very popular and tasty. Shrimp dust was sort of a byproduct of the drying process. Shrimp dust was used as fertilizer and feed. It was high in protein. Approximately 99% of the processed oysters and shrimp were shipped away on train from Houma. Most dried shrimp shipped out in big wooden barrels that weighed about 200 pounds.

For those who did not make their living by hunting and fishing, there was a work on the land. With help in short supply, plantations owners eagerly accepted the manual labor of the poor simple folks living between the plantation fields and the bayous.

Although sugarcane was the most profitable at the beginning of the 1900s, some plantation owners learned the value of rotating their crops. Thus, they grew Irish potatoes, sweet potatoes, peas, onions, corn, and beets. Most people that worked as pickers on plantations were not paid in cash. In exchange for their labor, they were paid in with whatever crops they were harvesting. Those fortunate to be paid in cash usually earned around 35 cents a day. Harvesting work was long and hard from before sunrise until well after sundown.

Some plantations had stores nearby that carried just about everything that could not be locally produced from hardware, shoes, dresses, jewelry, and dry goods by 100lb sacks. Most stores would divide the large sacks of dry goods into paper bags so each of those would come up to 10 to 15 cents. Traveling peddlers were a common site along the various bayous. They were often selling books, clothes, sausage, ham, and fruit.

Generous Louisiana nature had various resources to help making life better and supply the basic needs of the population. Palmetto (or small palm) grew wild and was abundant in low wetlands of south Louisiana. Like any other culture, the Cajuns made good use of all of their natural surroundings. They made brooms, hats, baskets, even fences and parts of the roofing, and whatever else from palmetto to make life a little easier.

In addition to abundance of wild berries growing in the forests along the bayous, many people had fruit trees. Many varieties of fruit grown through seedlings–Navel oranges, Louisiana sweet Satsumas, and lemons—could be seen in people's front and back yards. Apples, pears, blueberries, bananas, and grapes growing along the bayous were also readily available for those who were not lazy to pick. One could buy a large bunch of fresh bananas for 25 cents.

Although most people living along the bayous were very poor financially, they were ready to support and help each other. If someone said they would be somewhere to help, they were there no matter what—come hail or high water. If someone was in bind, the neighbors got together and helped. In many cases, one did not even need to ask. As people traveled up and down the bayous on their daily business, they would often stop to help others. It was just something what people did and expected to do without question.

Instead of convenient electrical washers and dryers doing laundry for us today, people at the brink of the 20th century commonly used wooden tubs and washboards at bayou's edge to wash their clothes. Homemade soap out of lard and lye successfully served the purpose of washing detergent.

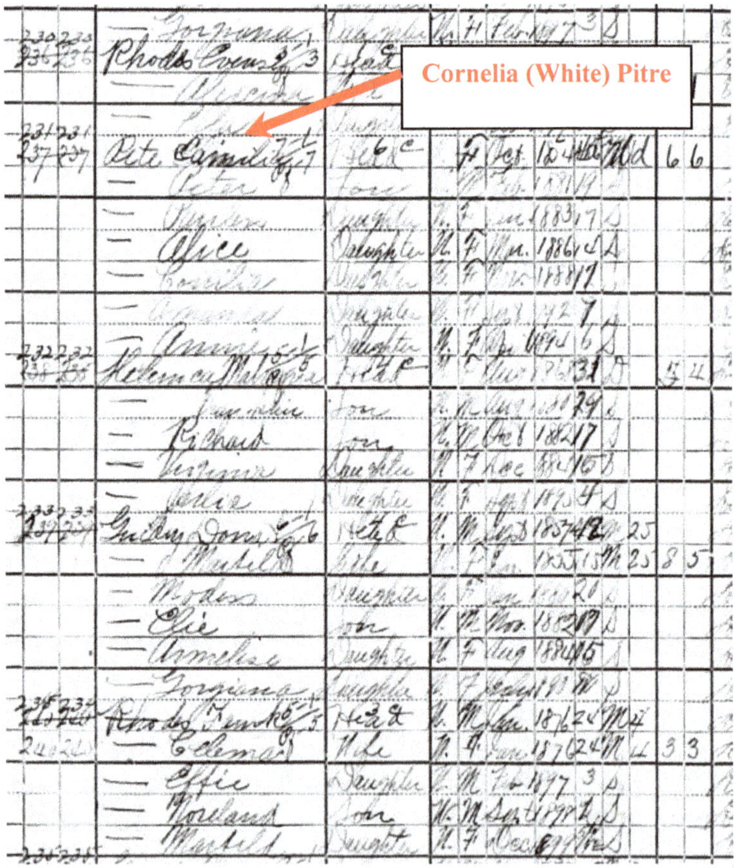

Life along the bayous for most was humble and simple. However, anyone willing to work could easily feed the family. With bountiful wild game, seafood, berries, and varieties of garden fruits, no one living along the bayou went hungry in the early 1900s.

The 1900's census documented widow Camilia

Figure 17 : 1900 US Federal Census, Terrebonne Parish, Sheet #14

Pete [sic] [26] (A.b. 1854) (Cornelia Mathilda (White) Pitre) still living along the lower Bayou Terrebonne just before Bayou LaCache, south of Montegut. Her homestead was listed as the tenth after her son Lenius Élie (b.1878; 8-III) and forth after John (A.b.1876 8-II). At the age of 46, after her husband passed away in 1898, she decided not to remarry and chose to continue with her life along the bayou community to finish raising her children. Peter (b.1880; 8-IV) (Richard Peter) was now 19 and an oyster fisherman like his father. The other children living with their mother were Camilia (b.1888; 8-VII) [sic] (Cordelia Camilia b.11/1888), 12, Amanda (b.1892; 8-VIII) (Amanda Josephine "Mandy," b. 9/1892), 7, and Ammerice (b.1895; 8-IX) [sic] (Mary Amy Annie, b. 4/1895), 6. Also living with them were Paulon (b.1883), 17, and Alice (b.1886), 14. The latter two were not referenced as Cornelia's children or grandchildren. Possibly they were her nephew and niece.

Here is an important notice regarding Daniel White and his change of name from Nettleton. The 1900's census lists them both: Daniel Nettleton, age 27, and Daniel White, age 51. Neither of these two men are Cornelia White's farther. The Daniel White listed here is Cornelia's older brother. The point is that in most censuses of LaFourche and Terrebonne parishes, both names of those men were recorded leading to the possibility of someone assuming the change of the name, but there was a 24-year age difference, and they could not possibly be the same person.

Figure 18 : Circa 1900, Common Sailing Skiff harvesting oysters

Élie Pete (Lenius Élie "Lee" Pitre) (b.1878; -), a 22 year-old oyster fisherman, had married Marie Lea Julienne Rhodes (b. June, 1872) on April 27, 1899. Their first child was

---

[26] Year: *1900*; Census Place: *Police Jury Ward 6, Terrebonne, Louisiana*; Roll: *584*; Page: *14A*; Enumeration District: *0074*; FHL microfilm: *1240584*.

deceased. He carved out his own family settlement up the Bayou not far from Daniel Nettleton and Daniel White's families.

During that time, Élie's [(b.1878; -)] older brother, John Lee Pitre [(A.b.1876 8-II)], 24, was also living a modest live along Bayou LaCache (lower Bayou Terrebonne). He was living three houses away up river from his mother Cornelia Pitre [(A.b.1854)]. His name was misspelled in the census as "John Pete". John Lee's house was listed as the fifth family settlement down river from Daniel White[27]. He was providing for his family by harvesting oysters using one of the small sailing skiffs he had built himself. He would stay out for ten days at a time dredging for oysters before returning home. They were still living not far north from the thriving community at Sea Breeze, approximately 19 miles south of Montegut village as the bayou flows. His wife, Francis stayed at home taking care of their three young kids: Wisteria [(b1897; 9-I)], 5, Élie [(A.b.1898; 9-ii)], 3, my grandfather, and Howard [(b.1899; 9-III)] who was born 6 months earlier.

By 1905, John [(A.b.1876 8-II)] had become very prosperous. He had several people working for him, so he built a second house alongside of his for the workers to sleep. Both houses had two stories. Before 1909 hurricane, there were many large houses along lower Bayou LaCache. John also acquired a horse carrousel and set it up in his front yard along the bayou. For a nickel, you could ride the "flying" horses while enjoying mama's homemade ice-cream. At this point in my journey, I have not been able to pinpoint the carrousel in John's timeline. However, I am pretty sure it was destroyed in one of the storms in 1909 or 1926. According to Sherwin Guidry's publication in 1970, if you were at least 60 years old and from Montegut, you would remember John's horse carousel.

In 1908, Wisteria [(b.1897; 9-I)] was 11 years old and started helping her father with work. During this time, John [(A.b.1876 8-II)] found he could augment the cash he made from oysters as well as spend more time at home by building small flat bottom seining boats, pull poles, small sail boats, and paddles. He also made chords used for cordelling. Cordele is a heavy twisted rope for towing boats.

Wisteria [(b.1897; 9-I)] puttied nail holes and did some of the sanding. At first, her brother Élie [(A.b.1898; 9-II)] did not like helping with boats. John [(A.b.1876 8-II)] would use steam box on top of a large iron pot with water to steam heat plank to bend it. Since Cyprus trees were in abundance, he primarily used them. He would seal the cracks between the wood planks with heavy cotton laced with linseed oil. John used a special flat head tool to drive in the cotton into the cracks to stop water leakage.

---

[27] Year: *1900*; Census Place: *Police Jury Ward 6, Terrebonne, Louisiana*; Roll: *584*; Page: *13B*; Enumeration District: *0074*; FHL microfilm: *1240584*

Figure 19 : Lapeyrouse store, Dry shrimp Storage building

It was around this time when Ralph Élie Crawford came looking for John Pitre (A.b.1876 8-II) to build some skiffs. A skiff was a small row boat specially designed for use in the marsh and narrow bayous. Ralph was a full blooded Cherokee Indian, known as Chief War No Tee. He had blue eyes and long black hair braided down to his knees. At that time, the Crawfords owned "The Floating Palace" showboat in which they traveled along the bayous and rivers putting on vaudeville acts. Chief War No Tee (Ralph Crawford) was known for peddling his herbal Indian medicines along the Terrebonne waterways during the 1920s. The showboat's rout was from Cocoadrie to Houma, and to New Orleans. Later, John even built the houseboat that the Chief used. The Crawfords lived at John and Francis's house while their boats were being built. John built three skiffs for him. They would use the smaller skiffs to go fishing while they traveled in their showboat. During that time, Mr. Crawford acquired John and Francis's permission so their daughter Wisteria (b.1897; 9-I) could work for them doing routine house chores. Eventually, Wisteria (b.1897; 9-I) started performing in some of the vaudeville and magic shows on "Floating Palace" aka "Beatrice". She remembered the story that one time she did not pull her legs far enough and the heel of her shoes were sawed off during the trick.

According to Ralph Eli Crawford (b.1879; d.1929) WWI draft card, he was born June 30, 1879. The card described him as an Indian, tall, with brown eyes, and black hair. Ralph's occupation was working for a drug store called Indian Herbal Store that was situated on 1326 Dryades Street in New Orleans, LA.

In September of 1909, a tropical disturbance over the western Atlantic began[28]. By September 18, the hurricane had attained winds up to 100mph as it moved over

---

[28] Hurricane of 1909 http://en.wikipedia.org/wiki/1909_Atlantic_hurricane_season#Hurricane_Nine

western Cuba with South Central Louisiana in its sites. By September 21, hurricane hit near Grand Isle, Louisiana, as a powerful, category 3 storm with winds up to 120mph.

John Pitre [(A.b.1876; 8-II)] was still living a very prosperous life built along lower Bayou LaCache. Initially, he did not think the storm was going to be very bad. So he tied up his boats to the porch and told his family they would ride out the storm in their home. That afternoon the winds really started whipping up. The kids watched through the window while the horse carousel spun wildly and began breaking apart. By early that evening, just after dark, the water had already risen into the first floor of their home. John told his family they would simply wait it out in the attic of their two-story house. However, by midnight, water was well into the second floor and still rising. Once John realized the storm was far more serious than he first believed and that it was going to get much worse, he punched a hole through in the roof. He could see one of the boats he tied to the porch was still there. He quickly loaded his family into the boat. When another large wave hit, their boat was swept away, and they ended up across bayou Petit Caillou from the Chauvin Brother's store.

After the storm, they realized they had lost just about everything. Both of John's houses were completely gone along with everything in them[29]. The only thing they did not lose in that horrific storm was that boat in which they were riding out the storm. The only clothes they had left was what they wore at the moment. The storm even ruined all of John's oyster beds and one of his boats. Without anything of their own left, the Pitres settled in a government provided tent.

By the end of 1909, John [(A.b.1876 8-II)] left the government provided tents in Chauvin and sailed his boat back to Bayou Terrebonne in attempts to resettle his family there. Learning from the lessons of so many family settlements completely wiped out and lives lost, he decided to choose a place further up the bayou. This time, he chose to rent one of the battered houses right next to where Madison Canal intersected with Bayou Terrebonne. The house the Pitres were renting had significant damage from the same 1909 storm. Although the floor had fallen and the house had some damage from the storm, it was much better than living in tents.

---

[29] Wisteria Marie Pitre Carlos, "Mrs. Carlos Relishes Life", Interview, *The Courier*, Jan 6, 1981.

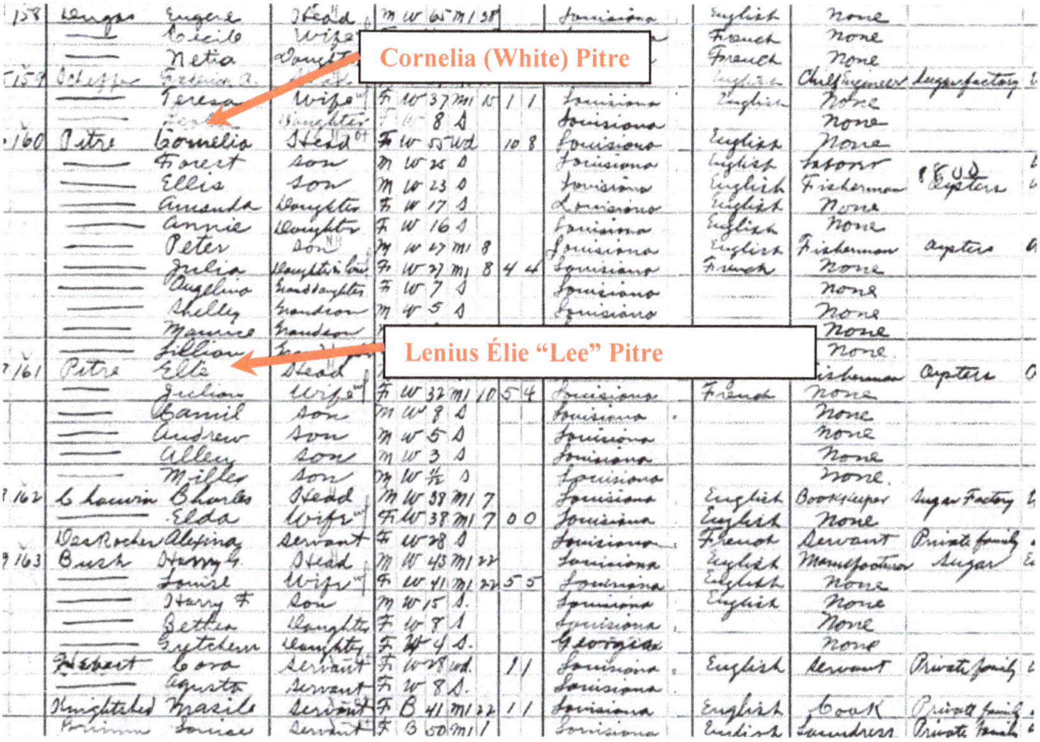

Figure 20 : 1910 US Federal Cencus, Terrebonne Prish, Ward 6, Sheet # 10

In 1910, Cornelia [A.b.1854] Mathilda (White) Pitre[30], 55, a widow of Élie Pitre

[A.b.1841, 7-IV], was listed as living along upper Bayou Terrebonne inside the Montegut village in district 108, ward 6. Eight of her ten children were still living. Residing with her was her son Forest[b.1883;8-V], 25, who was working as an oil field laborer; son Ellis[b.1885;8-VI], 23, oyster fisherman; daughter Amanda[b.1892;8-VIII], 17; daughter Annie[b.1893;8-IX], 16; son Richard[b.1880;8-IV] Pierre "Peter" Pitre, 27, oyster fisherman; Peter's wife, Julienne "Julia" (LeBouef), 27; Angelina, granddaughter, 7; Shelly, granddaughter, 5; Maurice, grandson, 3; and Lillian, granddaughter, 7 months. The family moved here from their homestead down lower LaCache Bayou after total loss during the 1909 storm.

By this time Lenius Élie "Lee" Pitre [b.1878; 8-III], 30, and his wife Marie Lea Julienne (Rhodes), 32, had four children: Camile, 8, Andrew, 5, Allen, 3, and Millar,

[30] Ancestry.com. *1910 United States Federal Census* [database on-line]. Provo, UT, USA: Ancestry.com Operations Inc, 2006. Index 1910, Louisiana, Terrebonne, Police Jury Ward 6, District 0108, Image 19, Lines 21-31

11 months. As most other men in the community did, Lenius [(b.1878; 8-III)] provided for his family as an oyster fisherman and trapper.

By 1910, John [(A.b.1876; 8-II)] and Francis's family grew to eight kids; Wisteria [(b.1897; 9-I)], 13, Élie [(A.b.1898; 9-II)], 11, Howard [(b.1899; 9-II)], 9, America [(b.1902; 9-IV)], 7, Emily [(b.1904; 9-V)], 4, Naise [(b.1906; 9-VI)], 3, Rosena [(b.1908; 9-VII)], 23 months. The family was still living along the Terrebonne bayou right next to Madison Canal. The census listed them in district 108 of ward 6 which was just south of Montegut in Terrebonne Parish.

Figure 21 : St. Martin and Co., Boudreaux Canal Store, Circa 1911

John [(A.b.1876; 8-II)], 30, was making enough money with various odd carpentry contracts that helped with renting the house and provided for his family.   Having lost almost everything in the storm including his oyster beds, he was happy to pick up any job. Since many people in the surrounding community that survived the storm also lost a lot, small skiffs and other wooden items necessary for fishing, shrimping, and crabbing were in big demand. Later John began building larger schooners.

John [(A.b.1876; 8-II)] and Francis just had another baby-girl, and there was no money coming in to buy milk and they did not own any cows. Wisteria [(b.1897; 9-I)] was 13 years old at the time and had to walk a few miles north through the swamp to watch some babies while the babies' mother milked the cows and tended to her daily chores. Wisteria [(b.1897; 9-I)] was paid one gallon of milk per day for the help. Since they did not have any refrigeration, after bringing milk home, Wisteria boiled and lowered it into well with a rope. It was the coldest place to keep perishable goods.

Wisteria [(b.1897; 9-I)], Élie [(A.b.1898; 9-II)], and Howard [(b.1899; 9-II)] used to pick live moss to sell. However, it had to be cured before anyone would buy it. The children would dig a hole in the ground and bury the moss. They would wet it every day until it turned gray. After that they would dry it in the sun until it turned black. Cured moss was commonly used in horse collars, pillows, mattress and furniture stuffing.

The Pitre children also caught and sold *les touloulous* "fiddler crabs" for 25 cents a basket. They removed claws and sold them to Linias Lapeyrouse to feed his turtles. Linias was a part-owner of a general merchandise store working together with his father in Montegut. He and another man from Grand Isle were the only ones to have the license to raise turtles in Louisiana. Linias raised terrapins, smaller species of turtle living in fresh or brackish water, which were trapped in spring through summer. The turtles were kept in special pits and fed. During winter they were shipped to Cheesebrough Brothers in New York.   Lapeyrouse and his partner usually shipped about 12 to 15 thousand of terrapins each season.

John's [(A.b.1876; 8-II)] was a very strict and religious man. He raised his children in an old stern fashion. He would get his family up at 3 a.m. to go to Saint John the Baptist Church by boat. The church was built in 1868 under the direction of Father Jean Marie Joseph Denece. It was completely destroyed in the 1909 storm. The church was located at the place where the present day Dugas Cemetery is situated. It was about 5.5 miles up Bayou Terrebonne from Madison Canal where the Pitre's lived. John almost never allowed his daughters to go to dances. Even when he did, they had to be chaperoned. Being raised with high moral values, his daughters were also forbidden to go swimming in public when boys were around.

When Mardi Gras time came, it was no exception. John [(A.b.1876; 8-II)] was unyielding about not permitting his children to dress up in costumes. "Mardi Gras" is French for "fat Tuesday". The holiday is celebrated on the last day before the Catholic Lenten season starts with Ash Wednesday. Tuesday is the last day of carnival celebrations. One long-standing tradition of the times for people on the lower bayous of south Louisiana is to travel down the bayous stopping at each house on their way to their final celebration party. Many of the travelers would give out candy and ask for various food items to contribute to the public meals. One such boat from New Orleans would always stop and give out more candy to John's children than to the other houses on the way down to their camp. Those people knew John and his family very well.

Once the Lenten season had ended, Cajuns celebrated Easter by decorating eggs with different color crepe paper. The local priest would scatter peas to trick children into believing it was the rabbit remains. The end of the year was marked by Christmas celebrations and festivities. John [A.b.1876; 8-II] and Francis used to hang stockings inside the house. They would fill them with candy, pecans, popcorn, and pecan pralines. In those older days, poor people did not decorate trees.

When Mr. Watkins found out that John [A.b.1876; 8-II] and Francis lost almost everything during the storm and saw the condition of the house they were renting, he offered them to live in one of his rent houses in Houma. He also brought boxes of clothes and shoes for them. Mr. Watkins knew John very well. Gilbert L. Watkins[31] owned lumber yard in Daigville where John would buy lumber for his boats. He was also Honorable Judge Louis Watkins's uncle. Daigville, as it was known during the time, was on the east bank of bayou Caine, just south of Houma city line.

By the time 1914 came around, Wisteria [b.1897; 9-I] turned 16 years old. The technology was still out of access for regular working people. The only phone around was at the store in Chauvin. One could buy a new Ford auto for $440 and a gallon of gas cost 13 cents. Average new homes were about $3,395 for those that could afford one. The annual income of the various laborers was about $1,257. With an income like that, the prices were unreachable for the typical Cajun living along the bayous of far south Louisiana.

It is interesting to note that because of the citrus canker eradication program in 1914-1930, the government uprooted the diseased trees and replaced them with canker resistant trees. After around 1919, most trees came from grafting.

During the winter of 1916, Wisteria [b.1897; 9-I] and her husband were living in Grand Caillou. Their first child was one and a half years old when John [A.b.1876; 8-II] and family got sick with flu. John [A.b.1876; 8-II] was living just south Montegut. Their house was the first after the Madison Canal bridge. That year's flu was dangerous, claiming up five or six people's lives daily.

In those days people used herbs and roots to treat different illnesses. Wisteria [b.1897; 9-I] had learned the old remedies from her grandmother, when she was 13 years old. She could make a special curing tea with leaves or roots of plants or peppermint. Tea to lessen headache and chills was made with orange flowers, and it would make one sleepy letting the body to get stronger while sleeping. Raquette cactus was used to draw pus from infection and to treat shrimp stings. They also said it was good to

---

[31] Year: 1900; Census Place: Police Jury Ward 3, Terrebonne, Louisiana; Roll: 584; Page: 3A; Enumeration District: 0069; FHL microfilm: 1240584; Gilbert L. Watkins → {Brother} Joseph Washington Watkins→ {Son} Judge Joseph Louis Watkins, Jr.

eat raquette cactus which grew plentiful near gulf. Cactus tea was also used to treat women with lower back pains and inflammation in kidneys.

On September 12, 1918, Élie Joseph Pitre [A.b.1898; 9-II], like every other young man, registered for the draft. The WWI draft card described him as follows: age 20, 5'0" tall, of medium build, with light brown hair, and blue eyes. He listed his occupation as deckhand for Laurence F. Hebert on Brooklyn Ave in Houma. Élie specified that he was still living with his parents along the bayou in Montegut. His younger brother, Joseph Howard Pitre [b.1899, 9-III], also had a WWI draft card which listed him as short height, medium build, with gray eyes, and brown hair.

1920s

In 1929, D.J. Theriot was in Biloxi, Mississippi, looking to buy a shrimp trawl. This would be the first one in Petit Caillou. While being there, he witnessed a shrimp fleet blessing. Around 1930, the first shrimp fleet blessing was held in Louisiana on the banks of

Figure 22 : Circa 1920s, Boyne General Store & Ship Yard, Madison Canal

Boudreaux Canal next to Avis Duplantis's meat market.

As many other farmers in Louisiana, Chauvin brothers rotated crops on their land—cotton, sweet potatoes, Irish potatoes, sugar cane, beans, and beets—for better harvest. It was common for locals to use the corn silk for pillows and mattresses, but it had to be re-stuffed twice a year. Many people grew their own corn, potatoes, and peanuts to get through winters easier. Those that had money or goods to trade would buy potatoes by the sack. Many reused the sacks as doormats or even clothing items. It was common to see locals washing their clothes with homemade soaps during the day at the bayou by pounding them with their hands.

By 1920 John Pitre [A.b.1876; 8-II] moved his family from that storm that ravished rental house south of Montegut to Houma. Their new house was owned by Gilbert L. Watkins, and it was in much better condition. The census listed him living in district 98 of ward 7 in Terrebonne Parish. He was 46 years old and still supporting his family by doing odd carpentry jobs and building various boats. Due to the rising population, the need for carpenters was increasing. Wisteria had married James Carlos [b. 1889] and moved to Grand Bayou.

John [A.b.1876; 8-II] and Francis still had eight children living under their modest roof. Élie [A.b.1898; 9-II], 22, was working with his father taking on whatever carpentry jobs that came along their way. Howard [b.1899; 9-III], was 21 and worked as a coastal fisherman. The rest of the children were Emily [b.1904; 9-V], 16, Anaise [b.1906; 9 -VI], 14, Rosana [b.1908; 9-VII], 12, Eldora [b.1912; 9-IX], 7, Francis [b.1914; 9-X], 5, and Johnny [b.1817; 9-XI], 2. Their mother, Francis (Autin), was 43 and most certainly had her hands full helping her husband feed and care for such a large family.

John Lee Pitre [A.b.1876; 8-II] was unable to read or write. He never attended any form of public or private schooling. However, he was a talented carpenter able to create various wooden household necessities as well as all kinds of boats. Without making paper drawings, John simply kept all of the designs in his head. John's [A.b.1876; 8-II] love of the bayou as well as his lively hood could not keep him in Houma for long.

Approximately in 1921, John Pitre [A.b.1876; 8-II] purchased land around the two large oak trees on the left (east) bank of Bayou Petit Caillou. Those were the same two oak trees where his brothers and he would sometimes stop and rest during their occasional trips up the bayou. Unfortunately, the house John lived in 1920s has been torn down shortly after 1965, and I was not able to acquire any pictures. However, I established the place where it was located – across the bayou (from the present day Lashbrooke Street). It was that place where he started to work on developing his successful boat building business. Although that house was gone long time ago, another house built by John [A.b.1876; 8-II] for one of his daughters still sits on a lot right next door.

John [A.b.1876; 8-II] built the first boat that used to ferry kids to school; it was named "The World". Unfortunately, I was not able to locate any pictures of the boat or determine the year it was built.

Figure 23 : Children riding boats to school, Circa 1930

In January of 1921, Élie Pitre (A.b.1898; 9-II) married Leona A. LeBoeuf in Houma. Leona was only a couple years younger than Élie (A.b.1898; 9-II). She was born on January 30, 1900 in Montegut. Her parents were Beattie Paul LeBoeuf and Olympia Aimee Hebert.

Élie (A.b.1898; 9-II) acquired some property around 1921 and built the house himself. It was located on the southern corner of Jerry Ann Street and Highway 56, known at the time as Little Caillou Road. The house was torn down sometime during 2011. By the late 1920s, Élie (A.b.1898; 9-II) and Leona had three children: the oldest was Wilbert (b.1923; 10-I) born on March 7, 1923; the middle was Doris (b.1926; 10-II) born in January, 1926; and the youngest Lee Roy (A.b.1928; 10-III), born on April 12, 1928. The youngest Élie's son, Lee Roy J. Pitre (A.b.1928; 10-III), is my father. He was born in Houma, Louisiana, and had hazel blue eyes and black hair.

Also around 1921, Charles "CD" Long, a German immigrant, came to Chauvin looking for John Pitre (A.b.1876; 8-II) because he heard about him being boat builder and wanted a paddlewheel showboat. He lived with John and Francis while the showboat was being built. John (A.b.1876; 8-II) was 46 years old when he finished building the showboat. In 1922, CD Long ended up marring one of John's daughters, Emelie Marie Pitre (b.1904; 9-V). Their first child, Emeline (b.1923; 10-I) was born on showboat about a year later.

The showboat was lined with wallpaper. It had five rooms on two stories. A parlor, guest room, dining room, kitchen, and master bedroom were on the second floor. The showroom was on the first floor. The boat had three bathrooms for convenience of the passengers. The owners charged 50 cents for a guest to sleep on the boat overnight. CD Long died during 1928 of pneumonia in New Orleans. The performance on the boat cost 25 cents per person. They usually had vaudeville shows, magic acts, and singing. The passengers could also buy peanuts on the boat and travel throughout the bayous of south Louisiana down to New Orleans. Many showboats existed at the time throughout the Mississippi River Valley. CD and his wife were successful with their boat; they eventually acquired three tents and multiple trailers. They even had separate crews which would work shows in different places at the same time. In one of their magic shows, Emelie [b.1904; 9-V], CD's wife, participated in magic tricks and used to be "sawed" in half.

Before 1926, the cypress and oak forests all throughout lower Terrebonne Parish were so lavish and thick; one could not see Montegut lights from Little Caillou. Today the landscape picture is very different – very few trees remain in the area due to salt water encroachment and the lights of Montegut are easily seen from Chauvin at night.

On September 20, 1926, Great Miami Hurricane hit Pensacola stalling in the area for a day. After that the storm headed east, towards Louisiana shores. John Pitre's [A.b.1876; 8-II] family again took refuge in his boat in Bayou Petit Caillou. When a 15-foot storm surge roared right through lower Terrebonne parish, many boats and homes were destroyed. The storm of 1926 put an end to all settlements along lower Bayou Terrebonne, south of Madison Canal.

It is believed that around 1929, John Pitre [A.b.1876; 8-II] built the first boat in Chauvin that had a motor, but I have not been able to verify it. The story tells that it was Phillis Ellender's second boat built by John that had the first motor along Bayou Petit Caillou.

When finally the majority of Cajuns were well settled in south Louisiana, history proved that their hardships were far from over. The Great Mississippi Flood of 1927 was the most destructive river flood in United States history.

In attempts to save the imminent flooding of New Orleans and despite the objections of many, Governor O.H. Simpson took the advice of his advisors and began making preparations. Over 10,000 people were evacuated along the river south of New Orleans. According to the Governor's plan, with 30 tons of dynamite, a Mississippi River levee at Caernarvon, Louisiana, was blown up. Much of St. Bernard and all of Plaquemines parish quickly flooded. That was the cost to protect New Orleans and spare it from serious damage. However, the destruction of the Caernarvon levee was unnecessary; several major levee breaks happened at that time in central Louisiana, including one the day after the demolitions.

On May 17, the Atchafalaya River breached the levee at Melville in Saint Landry Parish. The devastating waters rushed south to join with the flood waters from the Bayou des Glaises levee breach. When the two floods met, they combined flooding out Arnaudville, Breaux Bridge, New Iberia, Jeanerette, Franklin, and Morgan City. By the end of May, my grandparents on mother's side – Luke and Louise Theriot – along with my mother, who was less than 1 year old, joined 12,000 refugees in Lafayette. Prior to the flood, they were living between Breaux Bridge and Parks Louisiana. Once the flood waters started to recede over 10,000 square miles in 20 parishes were under water. In total, some 60,000 Louisianans became refugees living in various camps.

People had been promised full compensation for their losses. Still, very few received an average of $ 274 each, but many thousands of flood victims did not receive anything.   The financial leaders significantly underestimated the destruction and losses. The initial estimate was that the claims would be for the amount between two and six million dollars; however, the real numbers quickly grew to over 35 million dollars. Despite the efforts of local government and Red Cross, there were several reports of terrible living and sanitary conditions in various refugee camps.

Figure 24 : Blessing of the Fleet, Boudreaux Canal, Circa 1930

The flood and its aftermath resulted in a great cultural output of folklore and music and was a significant factor in the Great Migration by the thousands to Chicago and other northern cities. The US Congress acted and passed the 1928 Flood Control Act.

1930s

The Great Depression of the 1930s affected most of the world. However, the common people of lower Terrebonne Parish did not even know there was a depression. The working conditions were good, people were satisfied, and the parish's economy did not seem to be affected. Sugar cane plantations were thriving, and shrimp drying platforms operated full time. Most drying platforms worked 27 days a month with three days off. They had four or five workers per platform to buy shrimp from catchers, boil, and dry it on site.

Figure 25 : Circa 1930 Bayou Petit Caillou, facing LaCache Plantation

The 1930's census of Lafourche parish documented the widow Cornelia (White) Pitre [(A.b.1852)], 74, who was living with her widowed son-in-law Claude Naquin, 35, and his mother Josephine Naquin. There is no evidence proving when or why Cornelia [(A.b.1852)] decided to move in with her youngest daughter's family. Most likely it was after the devastation caused by the 1926 hurricane. 1930 brought yet another tragedy for Cornelia [(A.b.1852)], when she lost her youngest daughter Mary Amy "Annie" (Pitre) [(b.1893; 8-IX)], Claude's wife, on January 8. Annie was only 35, and the reason of her death is still unknown. She was married to Claude for about 14 years. The couple had two children: Elena, born in 1918 and Ruby, born in 1919.   Claude decided to burry Annie in Dugas Cemetery situated south of Montegut.

During the early 1930s, Cornelia [(A.b.1852)] (White) Pitre still had very long wavy hair. Her granddaughters remembered that her hair was so long that she could easily stand on its ends, and she was at least six feet tall. However, by that time her hair was mostly gray. Sometime in 1931, Cornelia decided to move back to Montegut and would live with her third born son's family. Lenius Élie Pitre [(b.1878; 8-III)] or Uncle Lee, as everyone called him, had recently purchased a large two-story house located on the east side of Bayou Terrebonne. The house was where current Montegut Street intersects with Highway 55 in Montegut. Élie [(b.1878; 8-III)] and his wife, Julienne, had nine children, so Cornelia spent her days helping around the house and being with her grandchildren. Her grandchildren would often talk about her love and pride in the bread she would bake for her family. Unfortunately, Élie's [b.1878; 8-III] children only had two years with their grandmother.

Cornelia [A.b.1852] was already senile with decreased heart function and chronic kidney infections. On March 21, 1934, my great-great grandmother was working in the garden, breaking old corn stalks so the peas could grow. She was bitten or stung by some kind of insect. Her already deteriorating body severely reacted to the sting. Cornelia's son, Lenius [b.1878; 8-III] took her to the emergency room where she was treated until she died on April 29. A copy of her death certificate was found at the Louisiana State Archives in Baton Rouge. Cornelia's grandchildren who I interviewed over the last couple of years described how the skin on the left side of her face and hands was black for several months. She was 81 and half years old when she died.

Early research, interviews[32] with living witnesses, and the funeral announcement made me think that Cornelia [A.b.1852] (White) Pitre was most likely buried in Claude Naquin's tomb at Dugas Cemetery in Montegut, Louisiana. Initially, this sounded plausible because according to the 1930's census[33] Cornelia [A.b.1852] was living with her son-in-law, Claude Naquin and his mother.

[32] Pitre, Lionel P. (2013,October). Personal interview.
[33] Year: 1860; Census Place: Ward 8, Terrebonne, Louisiana; Roll: M653_425; Page: 73; Image: 401; Family History Library Film: 803425

1—PLACE OF DEATH

MAY 12 1934   LOUISIANA STATE BOARD OF HEALTH
Bureau of Vital Statistics
CERTIFICATE OF DEATH 375

Parish   TERREBONNE

Police Jury Ward   6

Ward District No. 55-5537

File No. _____ (1, 2, 3, etc., in the order Certificates are filed.)

City or Town   MONTEGUT, LA.

Incorporated Town District No. _____ (Applies only to an incorporated town.)

Registered No. 4803 (To be given in Central Bureau.)

No. _____ St. _____ Ward (If death occurred in a Hospital or Institution, give its Name instead of Street and Number.)

2—FULL NAME   MRS. CORNELIA PITRE

(a) Residence. No. _____ MONTEGUT, LA. _____ St. _____ Ward. 6
(Usual place of abode)
Length of residence in city or town where death occurred. _____ yrs. _____ mos. _____ ds. How long in U.S., if of foreign birth? _____ yrs. _____ mos. _____ ds. (If non-resident give city or town and State)

PERSONAL AND STATISTICAL PARTICULARS   **MEDICAL CERTIFICATE OF DEATH**

3 SEX   FEMALE   4 COLOR OR RACE   WHITE   5 Single, Married, Widowed or Divorced (write the word)   WIDOWED

16 DATE OF DEATH   APRIL 29, 1934 (Month) (Day) (Year)

5a. If married, widowed, or divorced HUSBAND of (or) WIFE of   MR. ELIE PITRE

17 I HEREBY CERTIFY, That I attended deceased from MAR. 21, 1934 to APRIL 29, 1934
that I last saw h_____ alive on APRIL 29, 1934
and that death occurred, on the date stated above, at 11 A.M.
The CAUSE OF DEATH was as follows:
CHRONIC NEPHRITIS WITH HYPERTENSIVE MYOCARDIAL DECOMPENSATION (duration) _____ yrs. _____ mos. _____ ds.
CONTRIBUTORY (Secondary) 131 SENILITY.
(duration) _____ yrs. _____ mos. _____ ds.

6 DATE OF BIRTH (month, day, and year)   OCT. 12, 1852

7 AGE   Years 81   Months 6   Days 17   If LESS than 1 day, _____ hrs. or _____ min.

8 OCCUPATION OF DECEASED
(a) Trade, profession, or particular kind of work.
(b) General nature of industry, business, or establishment in which employed (or employer)   HOUSE WORK
(c) Name of Employer

18 Where was disease contracted, if not at place of death?   AT PLACE OF DEATH. XXX
Did an operation precede death? NO. Date of _____
Was there an autopsy? NO.
What test confirmed diagnosis? PHYSICAL FINDINGS
(Signed) JACOB O. HOTH (address)
19 (Address) MONTEGUT, LA.

9 BIRTHPLACE (city or town)   TERREBONNE PARISH
(State or country)

10 NAME OF FATHER   DANIEL WHITE

11 BIRTHPLACE OF FATHER (city or town)   TERREBONNE
(State or country)

12 MAIDEN NAME OF MOTHER   ELIZA PIERCE

13 BIRTHPLACE OF MOTHER (city or town)   TERREBONNE
(State or country)

*State the Disease Causing Death, or in deaths from Violent Causes, state (1) Means and Nature of Injury, and (2) whether Accidental, Suicidal or Homicidal. (See reverse side for additional space.)

14 Informant   SON—MR. LEE PITRE
(Address)

19 PLACE OF BURIAL, CREMATION, OR REMOVAL   MONTEGUT, LA.   DATE OF BURIAL 4-30-34

15 Filed _____ 30, 34 _____ Registrar

20 UNDERTAKER   CHAUVIN & BOURG.   ADDRESS HOUMA, LA

Eventually, I interviewed two of Cornelia's grandchildren who were doubtful she was buried in Naquin's tomb, but they could not remember much because they were only one and four years old at the time of her death.

When I first met Rosalie (Pitre) Crochet[34], we talked for several hours, and suddenly she presented me with a stunning revelation. There was still someone else much older living that had direct knowledge of Cornelia [(A.b.1852)]. Leola [(b.1916; 9-VII)] (Pitre) David, Rosalie's godmother, is in her late 90s and lives near New Orleans. Leola [(b.1916; 9-VII)] is one of Cornelia's granddaughters, and she was 18 years old when Cornelia [(A.b.1852)] died in 1934. Inspired by the new opportunity, I did not waste time and contacted Leola [(b.1916; 9-VII)] (Pitre) David to arrange a meeting. In October, 2013, I went to her home in Metairie, Louisiana, with high hopes of more revelations about my ancestors. Leola [(b.1916; 9-VII)] and some of her five generations of descendants were there eagerly waiting for my arrival.

---

[34] Crochet, Rosalie (Pitre) (2013, October). Personal interview

The 20th Century   Page 78 of 168

I was met by a short, 97 year-old woman with bright, lively eyes and a warm smile; she seemed to be in good health and spirits. During my first visit, she did not seem to remember much about her grandmother. However, Leola[35] was insistent that Cornelia was buried in the first row at Dugas Cemetery. She said that it was her father who made the coffin and brick tomb for Cornelia. Leola also remembered that there was only one open spot left in the first row of the cemetery, and her father took it to bury her grandmother. She also described the tomb as being low to the ground, but most likely caved in by now as with many of the tombs finished with the handmade bricks.

Later on, during our discussions back and forth about each other's family, Leola hit me with a striking newsflash. She said that Cornelia [(A.b.1852)] was six feet tall with blond hair and blue eyes. Upon further reflection, I realized that other interviewees stated that two of Cornelia's [(A.b.1852)] sons were about six feet tall as well as one of her surviving grandsons. This discovery led me to another question. Why was my great-grandfather (John Pitre [(A.b: 1874; 8-II)]) and all his male descendants averaging 5'2" and female descendants around 4'10"? I have yet to uncover any physical attributes about my great great-grandfather (Élie Pierre Pitre [(A.b. 1841 7-IV)]). A couple of explanations might be reasonable. Otherwise, there are only questions. Could a six-foot tall woman of English decent whose parents were reported to have some means, marry a 5'4" tall, literally dirt poor fisherman from the bayous of south Louisiana? Were both Élie [(A.b. 1841 7-IV)] and Cornelia [(A.b.1852)] tall, and maybe Cornelia's or Élie's mother was very short? Also which side of the family did John's [(A.b: 1874; 8-II)] pure blond hair and blue eyes come from? Cornelia did have three daughters whose physical attributes are not known to me. For me, it is an interesting and perplexing puzzle, and I may not find the answers I am looking for, but I hope there might be some documents describing or providing hints about my great great-grandfather and his appearance.

On my next visit to Dugas Cemetery, I was better prepared to search the grave more thoroughly. Like Leola explained, I found Cornelia White's grave in the front row; it was the sixth grave to the left of the main arch gate. Her son, Lenius Élie Pitre [(b.1878; 8-III)] built her coffin out of cypress board and laid the tomb with handmade bricks. The brick tomb eventually caved in, but someone covered the top with cement to help preserve it. It is very hard to read, but there is a small cement cross on top that reads "MS ELIE PITRE" with the birth and death years. Since the cross is made of cement that looks like a part of the new cement poured on top, it is probably not the original grave marker.

---

[35] Davis, Leola (Pitre) (2013, October). Personal interview

Figure 27 : Leona (LeBouef) Pitre circa 1930

Figure 26 : Francis (Autin) Pitre circa 1930

The 1930's census listed John Pete (sic) [(A.b.1876; 8-II)], 55, and his wife Francis, 54, as living in the unincorporated area of Chauvin, in ward 7 of Terrebonne Parish. His last name was misspelled in the census, but I am sure it was my great-grandfather. John and Francis's five children were recorded as residing with parents: Eldora M.[(b.1912;9-IX)], 17, Francis K.[(b.1914;9-X)], 15, John H.[(b.1917;9-XI)], 13, Cornelia G.[(b.1920;9-XII)], 9, and Marguerite [(b.1923;9-XIII)], 6. John [(A.b.1876; 8-II)] was still living in the house he built on the eastern side of Bayou Little Caillou. The value of the house was registered as $300. John declared that at the time he was a self-employed boat carpenter. It was at that location that John developed his boat building skills into a full time business.

My grandfather, Élie Joseph Pitre [(A.b.1898; 9-II)], 32 and first wife Leona, 30, were living in the house he built several years earlier along bayou Petit Caillou situated a short distance north of Saint Joseph Church. Élie's house valued at $250 was on the opposite side of the bayou from his parents, but a little further north. During that time, he was mostly working as a carpenter building boats. I have not found any information about the exact place where my grandfather worked, except that he was working as a contractor for one of the local boat building operations. Élie [(A.b.1898; 9-II)] and Leona's three children –Wilbert J. [(b.1923; 10-I)], 7 years old, Doris M. [(b.1926; 10-II)], 4 years, and Lee Roy J.[(A.b.1928; 10-III)], 23 months – still living in their parents' house.

In 1934, Lee Roy (A.b.1928 10-III), Wilbert (b.1923; 10-I), and Doris (b.1926; 10-II) together with their father faced a great personal tragedy when their mother died on August 8, 1934. Leona (A.b.1900) (LeBoeuf) passed away young, being only 34 years old. My father was six years old at the time. Élie Pitre (A.b.1898; 9-II) did not have money for the funeral, so he decided to sell his house to pay for his wife's burial. My father and his sister Doris (b.1925 10-II) moved in with their grandparents across the bayou. Wilbert (b.1923; 10-I) moved in with his Aunt America's (b.1902; 9-IV) family that was living several houses down from John (A.b.1876; 8-II) and Francis.

My father said he really did not remember much of his mother. He often said that he remembered that she died because of difficult times and hard work in the fields. However, his older cousin[36] Emeline (b.1923; 10-I) told me that Leona died of lung cancer. According to my father's military records, his mother died because of some kind of blood cancer. Leona was buried in the first row of the St. Joseph Cemetery in Chauvin. I am not sure in which tomb she is buried because I suspect her small granite marker has been moved around few times. Presently that marker sits on top of Maggie Richard's (1881-1940) tomb, and Maggie Richard is not related or associated with the Pitres.

Times were very difficult for the Pitre family living under poverty in the Deep South of Louisiana. Throughout his life, Lee Roy (A.b.1928 10-III) often told stories of hardships and how little they had even for daily necessities. The only reason he ever had meat to eat early in his life was because while living with his grandparents he kept a cage of wild birds. Those were mostly black birds and robins, and it was not illegal at that time. He caught them with homemade traps. I remember my Dad teaching me how to make such a simple trap out of small branches and string. His grandmother, Francis Autin, often cooked some of birds for them although she did not like the boys killing the birds to eat. A few of her granddaughters told me that she used to fuss about it in those days. She loved all kind of animals. Her grandchildren also remember how she would have a hug fit when her husband decided to get rid of several feral kittens that were hanging around the house and his sheds.

In 1937 Élie Joseph Pitre (A.b.1898; 9-II) married his second wife Aggie Marie Dupre (b.1911). Though, they never had any children together, and she died on August 21, 1951. Élie (A.b.1898; 9-II) would marry two more times; but his destined sad fortune was to outlive all four of his wives. His only three children came from the first marriage with Leona LeBoeuf.

---

[36] Cunningham, Emeline (Long), (April 30, 2013). Personal Interview.

1940s

According to the 1940's census records, John Pitre [(A.b.1876; 8-II)] was 65 and still living along the east bank of Bayou Petit Caillou near Chauvin. The little, one-room house he built before 1930 was increased in value to $300. At that time, John was building all kinds of boats with more orders than he could handle. Some of his nieces and nephews I interviewed shared stories from the old times and remembered how Uncle John was always busy when they came to visit. He would never stop working, even when he had relatives visiting. Francis, being 64 year old, still stayed at home helping with some of the grandkids. At that time, one of her daughters, Eldora, 26, worked as a laborer pealing shrimp in a local factory. Marguerite turned 16 and was staying at the parents' house.

Sometime during the early 40's Francis [(A.b.1879)] Pitre had a severe stroke and could no longer take care of herself. John quit working to help taking care of his wife. Wisteria [(b.1897;9-I)] would often come over from where she lived with her husband on Bayou Grand Caillou to help caring for her mother while her father worked on building whatever boat orders he had. However, shortly afterwards he stopped building boats and never started up again.

Among the family, relatives, and friends, John [(A.b.1874; 8-II)] was known for always having a cigar in his mouth or hand. One of his nephews told me he never took a whole one. He would use a small hatchet to cut cigars in half. The same hatchet he used to shave and break open oysters.
Although the handle was possibly replaced a few times, the hatchet in Figure 5 was at least 100 years old when my second cousin showed it to me in 2013.

John [(A.b.1874; 8-II)], would drink at least one glass of wine a day as ordered by doctor for high blood pressure. For Sunday meals, he had a tradition where everyone at the table would get one glass of Morgan David Concord Wine. I also remember a story of him taking a jug of wine with him when he went to work in the fields. One has to understand that people had only two sources of water along the bayou – either from

Figure 28 : Quentin Cunningham, Wilbert Pitre, Élie Pitre - circa 1947

hand dug wells or the bayou itself. People learned that it was better to drink from a distilled source so they did not get sick. Locally distilled ale or wine in those times was not as high in alcohol content as it is today, but much safer than raw water.

The 1940's census also listed Élie Joseph Pitre [A.b.1898; 9-II] at the age of 42, still living on upper Bayou Petit Caillou in ward 7 of Terrebonne Parish. He was now renting a house along upper Bayou Petit Caillou for $9 a month. It was from those census records that I discovered my grandfather had completed four years of formal education. I have not been able to find out which school he attended. It is likely that it must have been somewhere down lower Bayou Terrebonne. He stated that he was working as a contractor boat builder with an annual income of $800. He also listed his second wife Aggie, who was 29 years old. All three of the children were also recorded as residing with him and Aggie. His oldest son, Wilbert [b.1923; 10-I], 17, was working as a deckhand for Voohies tug boat pulling sugar cane barges. Doris [b.1925; 10-II] turned 14, and Lee Roy [A.b.1928; 10-III] was 12. From those records, it appears as if Élie's children came back to live with their father. To remind, they were living with their grandparents for a while after the children's mother Leona LeBouef [A.b.1900] passed away.

While working in Houma Wilbert Pitre [b.1923; 10-I] met Hilda Boudelouche [b.1921]. In November, 1941, just two weeks before Japan attached Pearl Harbor, they were married in Houma and initially settled in a small modest house in Houma on Pitre Street. A few years later, they moved into a house on Airport Road along the Vermillion River in Lafayette.

Around 1942, Wilbert [b.1923; 10-I] started working alongside with his father as a contract boat builder along upper Bayou Petit Caillou. Some of the boats they built were ordered by Quentin Cunningham for one of his side ventures. At the time Quentin was the director of Lafayette's Fleet

Figure 29 : Lee Roy Pitre, Sr. Circa 1943

Maintenance. Quentin quickly realized Élie [(A.b.1898; 9-II)] and Wilbert's [(b.1923; 10-I)] gifted skills in building boat hulls. He decided to expand his boat building venture by starting a partnership with them. In 1943, Cunningham-Pitre Shipyard partnership was formed between Quentin, Élie, and Wilbert. Quentin fronted the initial investment, and they purchased land along the Vermillion River in Lafayette immediately south of the Airport Road bridge. There were three houses already there on the property, so the Pitre's took residence there next door to the newly formed shipyard. There, along the Vermillion River bank and near present day General Mouton Bridge, over the next nine years the partners build many boats. All of their boats were built out of wood and at first were mostly smaller crew boats. In 1947 they landed an order for something a little larger. That was the first full size modern shrimp boat to be built in Lafayette. It was named the "Sally Gayle".

Figure 30 : Cunningham Pitre Shipyard - Mid 1940's

In 1946, my father, Lee Roy [(A.b.1928; 10-III)], also decided to stop working as a deckhand on shrimp boats; instead he wanted to work together with his father and brother building boats at the shipyard in Lafayette.

During the World War II, work at Cunningham-Pitre Shipyard came to a standstill. Like many skilled craftsmen who stayed behind, Élie [(A.b.1898; 9-II)] and his eldest son Wilbert along with a couple of his nephews, Cyrus LeCompte and Easton LeCompte, built boats for Higgins in New Orleans. At that time, Higgins was paying $1.50 an hour for skilled carpenters. Élie [(A.b.1898; 9-II)] never owned a car and rode to New Orleans with his nephew, Cyrus LeCompte. Wilbert [(b.1923; 10-I)] had his own car and would drive himself. They would drive from Lafayette to the Higgins boat yard in New Orleans and spend the work days over there, coming back to Lafayette for the

Figure 31 : Lee Roy Pitre, Sr. - Circa 1947

weekends.

I have not found any information pointing to where they slept while working for Higgins. I tend to believe that Higgins Industries did provide some temporary living quarters for their workers. Initially when they arrived, everyone was locked in and not allowed to leave for over a month due to national security. Their families did not know where they were or what happened since no one was allowed to even make any phone calls.

One evening on the plant floor, when everyone had gone home for the evening, Wilbert [(b.1923; 10-I)] stayed a little later as usual. Suddenly, he heard a voice yelling out to him from the offices upstairs and telling him to come up. It was Andrew Higgins himself. He wanted to know why Wilbert was still there working when everyone else had left for the day. Wilbert began to explain he was sharpening his tools and getting ready for the next day. Higgins then exclaimed he liked Wilbert's work ethics. Thus, unexpectedly, at the age of 17, Wilbert was promoted by Higgins to foreman[37]. This resulted in significant resentment by most of the older skilled workers. However, Wilbert was determined to succeed and worked diligently; his skills and work ethics helped him forging his confidence and eventually owning a shipyard of his own.

During my research journey, I stumbled across a few interesting stories as well as bits of fascinating information. About a year ago, I was trying to track down details on which school my Dad, Lee Roy Pitre, Sr. [(A.b.1928; 10-III)] attended in hopes of finding some pictures of that school. One of my assistant researchers tracked down someone who said the school burned down because a student put too much wood in the pot belly stove. So with that new detail, I kind of forgot about my quest to find pictures and moved on to focus on researching other pressing clues.

Later on, when in February of 2014 I was interviewing one of my older first cousins, who also happened to be my father's Godson, he suddenly remembered a story my Dad told him first hand many years ago. He said my father claimed to have burned down the school. He said it was cold winter along Bayou Petit Caillou, and he was tired of making trips to put wood in the heater. Therefore, he decided to put more wood, and it caused the stove to overheat. The fire started as a result of overheating. With such a shocking revelation, I immediately changed gears and focused on trying to find other potential witnesses who could provide some personal accounts of what happened and find out whether it was really my Dad who burnt the school.

---

[37] Bryan Pitre, Sr. (b.08/02/1945), Interview 02/08/2014

At first, several different stories emerged. Everyone described school as the building that had multiple rooms. There was a wood burning heater in the cloak room, so the heater was not in the classroom. Some witnesses claimed it was a group of boys messing around in the cloak room. Others insisted it was Lawrence Authement, Jr. who put too much wood in the heater. While attending a funeral for my second cousin's mother-in-law on

Figure 32 : LaCache School Circa late 1920s, Chauvin Village

February 14, 2014 in Chauvin, I decided to conduct a few more individual interviews on various subjects.

I was at Meryl Lapeyrouse's house, and she claimed that there were two different fires that burned down older LaCache school buildings. However, she did not remember any details as to the events. She did think she had a picture of the school. While she was looking through her binders and photo albums trying to find the picture, she stumbled across a picture she forgot she had. It was of my Dad and his best friend. Just so happened my Dad's best friend once dated Meryl in the early 1940s and must have given that picture to her. It was taken in a photo booth located at the baseball field in lower Chauvin. Meryl assured that Iris Marin, my Dad's friend from the picture, was still living in upper Chauvin. We quickly tracked down his phone number, and he excitedly granted me an interview. I met Iris and his gracious wife at their home. He did not remember taking that picture but both him and his wife said no doubt that was him in the picture.

Eventually, I turned the conversation towards the various stories I read about the school burning down. He suddenly said that he was actually present in the room at the time when the fire started. It was a bunch of boys in the cloak room where the wood heater was located. They put so much wood in it, the entire heater turned red from the bottom all the way up to the ceiling, and then the entire building caught on fire. Iris confirmed that it was not the two-story wooden school. It was the one story multi-room school that was off the ground on blocks.

Later, during 1944 with the WWII at its peak, Lee Roy Pitre, Sr. [A.b.1928; 10-III] wanted to join the Army, but he was only 16, and his farther would not sign his enlistment papers. Finally, Lee Roy, Sr. dropped out of school in 1947, halfway through the eighth grade and never returned to school. That decision he would later admit he regretted for the rest of his life. He decided he wanted to make a little money, so he could buy some decent cloths to go to the dances and not be embarrassed in front of the girls. Many of the local girls talked of how good a dancer he was.

At first, Lee Roy, Sr. took a job as a deckhand on a shrimp boat down the Bayou Petit Calliou. I do not know which boat or who owned it. He occasionally talked about his adventures but not in detail. Lee Roy [(A.b.1928; 10-III)] stated he never got paid any money for his time on the shrimp boat. My Dad's first cousin, Cyrus Pitre[38], told me the owner of the shrimp boat would give the money to my grandfather instead. My dad also once told me he really was not concerned about not being paid, he was as happy as can be because he was out on his own enjoying the adventures of travel on the open waters and for the first time in his life had all the fresh seafood he wanted to eat. This seemed like a luxury to him compared to the life of poverty he left behind.

After the WWII Élie [(A.b.1898; 9-II)], Wilbert [(b.1923; 10-I)], and Lee Roy [(A.b.1928; 10-III)] lived in two houses that were on the Cunningham Pitre Shipyard property in Lafayette. There was also an unoccupied old three story house on the property. It was torn down and with the salvaged wood, in 1951 Wilbert [(b.1923; 10-I)] and Élie completed building their homes and moved them to where they would settled down along Bayou Carlin.

Around 1945, John [(A.b.1876; 8-II)] Pitre, Sr. (my great-grandfather) built another house on his lot next door to his for his youngest daughter Marguerite and her husband.

---

[38] Cyrus Pitre, Interview 02/16/2014

Figure 33 : (left) Lee Roy Pitre, Sr. (right) unknown - circa 1946

       Élie Pitre [(A.b.1898; 9-II)] as many others in the Deep South took whatever odd jobs that were available to support his family. As I previously mentioned, he even worked building Patrol Torpedo (PT) boats during World War II. Élie [(A.b.1898; 9-II)] made most of his hand tools. Once he made an electric band saw out of parts he either fabricated or acquired. Eventually, Élie [(A.b.1898; 9-II)] settled into building shrimp boats full time. He later started a tradition—in each boat he built he would throw a penny in the bow.

While working at the Cunningham-Pitre Shipyard in Lafayette at the age of 20, Lee Roy Pitre [A.b.1928; 10-III] decided to join the Louisiana Army National Guard. He took his oath of enlistment on March 1, 1948, and started his military career as an infantry cook. Initially, he was paid about $10 for a standard weekend drill.

By December of 1948, he was quickly promoted to the rank of Corporal (SP2). On March 2, 1949 he was

Figure 34 : Cunningham Pitre Shipyard - circa 1947

the 156 Infantry Battalion. During 1954 he was chosen and assigned to manage the battalion's motor pool maintenance shop. In the late 1950s, he was assigned the title of Battalion Maintenance Instructor.

Figure 35 : Lee Roy Pitre, Sr. 2nd from left. Circa 1949

Figure 36 : John & Francis Pitre's Daughters - Francis, Eldora, Rose, Anna, Anaise, Emelie, America, Wisteria

1950s

On December 4, during the cold winter of 1953, Francis Marie [(A.b-1879)] Pitre finally passed away. After her stroke in 1943, she could not take care of herself and kept feeling worse despite her children and husband trying to do their best providing the necessary care. She was buried in St. Joseph Cemetery in Chauvin, Louisiana, in the first row in the tomb close to her husband John Lee Pitre [(A. b. 1876; 8-II)] who would outlive his wife for twelve years. It is said[39] that during her 74 years of life she gave birth to fourteen children. However, I have only been able to verify the names of thirteen of them. Most likely, at least one child died very young.

John Lee Pitre, [(A.b.1876; 8-II)] continued building boats and other carpentry jobs until his late 70s. John passed away while living with his youngest daughter in New Orleans on August 4, 1965.

Figure 37 : John Lee Pitre circa 1950s

---

[39] Cunningham (Long), Emeline, Chauvin Louisiana, Personal Interview, April 30, 2013

Figure 38 : Cunningham-Pitre Shipyard, Delcambre, Circa 1950s

By 1952 Cunningham-Pitre Shipyard had relocated from Lafayette to the property Wilbert previously purchased in Delcambre later in 1951. Wilbert and Hilda had already moved into the house that Wilbert had just previously built in Lafayette. Élie Pitre [A.b.1898; 9-II] purchased property from Isadore Delcambre on November 29, 1952. There he moved one of the three houses they built in Lafayette.

Eventually, Wilbert stepped in to run the family business when Élie [A.b.1898; 9-II] decided to retire. In 1972 Wilbert bought out Cunningham's share of the company and registered Pitre Shipyard, Inc. with the Louisiana Secretary of State.

Figure 39 : Wilbert Pitre, Quentin Cunningham, Élie Pitre, Cunningham-Pitre Shipyard, Delcambre, Circa 1950s

While working in Lafayette and attending as many dances as he could, Lee Roy Pitre [(A.b.1928; 10-III)] met Betty Jane Fabacher. Betty was born on November 6, 1933 that made her five years younger than Lee Roy. Lee Roy wanted to build his life and family in a slightly different way than his older brother.

In 1950 Lee Roy [(A.b.1928; 10-III)] married Betty Jane Fabacher. The following year she gave birth to a daughter. I do not have information regarding their first years of marriage. Nonetheless, sometime in 1954, Lee Roy settled with his wife and daughter into a house he purchased at 201 Norine Street on the northwestern side of Lafayette.

According to Lee Roy's military records in 1951, he had been working at Cunningham-Pitre Shipyard in Lafayette for about three years, and was making $40/week.

Sometime between 1952 and 1953, work at the shipyard in Delcambre was slow, so Lee Roy [A.b.1928; 10-III] took a temporary job at a gas station on University Street near Four Corners in Lafayette. A few months later, he landed a job building houses for $80 per week in Lafayette area. I have not yet been able to find out who was his employer were at that time.

In 1954 Lee Roy [A.b.1928; 10-III] had not yet specialized as a cabinet builder. He was still working as a carpenter building houses in the Lafayette area. During this time, while on one of his military drills, he requested a transfer to the motor pool. On February 28, 1954, at the age of 26, he was officially assigned to the Battalion motor pool as Wheel Vehicle Mechanic (MOS.1014). By this time, he was 185 lbs., and according to the military requirements, he was overweight. However, he was granted a waiver signed by the Battalion's General. During several of his training exercises, he was awarded Marksman and Expert with the 30-caliber M1 carbine rifle.

On May 30, 1957 group of workers split off to form Top's Woodwork & Supply, Inc. My Dad started working with them as a cabinet builder earning $85 a week. He enjoyed his free time away hunting and fishing. In fact, he built his own first trawling boat out of wood sometime around 1956. It was a small modest boat, but it met the family's need for fresh seafood all year round.

By 1957, Lee Roy [A.b.1928; 10-III] was separated from his first wife. It is unknown where he was

Figure 40 : Lee Roy Sr., Debra, David, Sr., Lawrence, Brian Sr., Élie

living at that period of time. He continued working at Top's in Lafayette. At the time, the company was located on Johnston Street. Possibly, he also worked part-time at the shipyard in Delcambre.

By the end of the 1950's, Élie Pitre [A.b.1898; 9-II] was far less involved in building boats and started to settle down into enjoying his retirement years. Élie would spend the bulk of his time in Delcambre socializing with friends and family. To make the best of the time at hands, he decided to recreate a large model of one of the last shrimp boats he built, "Captain Abbie". The model was eventually given to the owner of the actual shrimp boat, Captain "Abbie" Anthony Pierre, Abbie, who proudly displayed the model in his front yard for many years. However, due to weather and lack of proper care, the wooden model eventually rotted beyond saving.

Figure 41 : Élie Pitre posing with Model shrimp boat he built, circa 1960

1960s

According to the document records, as of January 3, 1960 Lee Roy (A.) still worked as cabinet maker for Top's Woodwork & Supply for $85/week. The company was located on Johnston Street, behind present day La Fonda's restaurant.

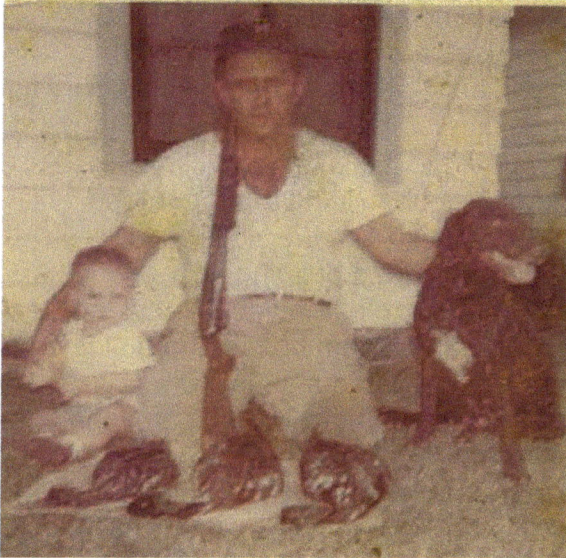

While still living in Lafayette, Lee Roy Pitre (A.b.1928; 10-III) married his second wife in February 1960, the former Lou Anna Theriot (A.) of Parks, Louisiana. They decided to settle in a small modest home that Anna Lou had previously purchased. This small house still exists today and located on Doc Duhon Rd. on the north side of the Lafayette, Louisiana. Shortly after the birth of their first child, Lee Roy J. Pitre, Jr. (b. 1960; 11-II), on July 14, 1960, being a healthy 6 lbs. 8½ oz. child, his father changed his name to Lee Roy J. Pitre, Sr. (A.b.1928; 10-III).

Figure 42 : Lee Roy, Sr., Jr., &

In early 1961, because of the Berlin Wall crisis, rumors started spreading among the National Guard that they were going to be activated. Lee Roy (A.b.1928; 10-III) was thinking about his son who just turned one year old and was afraid that the boy would not recognize him when he returned from overseas. So he decided to resign from the National Guard and was granted an honorable discharge on May 15, 1961.

At that time he had attained the rank of (E6) SSG and was assigned to 3628th Ordinance Company of the 156th Infantry brigade as automotive repair inspector (with a specialty code of 635.60 that the Army designates for the skill of automotive repair inspector). At that time he could make about $30 per the four-day weekend drill.

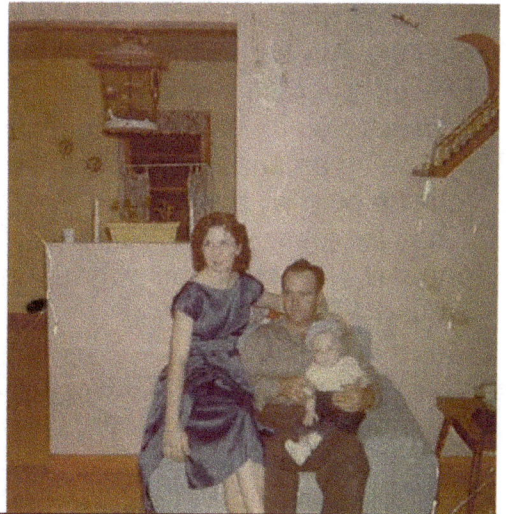

I never had the privilege of getting to know my great-grandfather. From researching surviving details about his life, it is clear that he was not only a hardworking man living along the Bayous and Marshes of South Louisiana; he was a very proud man of high ethics and morals. John Lee Pitre [A. b: 1874; 8-II], died on August 4, 1965, soon after my fifth birthday.

Paying credit to his legacy, I would like to remind that he could not read or write nor did he have any formal education. Nevertheless, his illiteracy did not stop him from being a skilled and talented boat builder who was well respected among the community. During the great flu epidemic I discussed earlier, he even would sometimes take wood off the side of his house to build coffins to help people bury their loved ones.

Early on, John [A. b: 1874; 8-II], learned the basics of building a pirogue and bateaux as well as making cast and seining nets, from his farther, Élie [A.b. 1841; 7-IV] Pierre Pitre. After Élie married Cornelia [A.b.1852] and started building his new homestead on the banks of Bayou Terrebonne, just south of Madison Canal, he learned some rudimentary skills of wood bending using steam boxes and building of sailing skiffs from the Boyne family who owned and operated a shipyard a few hundred yards up the bayou at Madison Canal from his homestead. Once John settled on his own homestead in 1873 on Lower Bayou LaCache after marrying François, he advanced his carpentry skills building larger boats by learning from the Rhodes family, who had their own shipyard a few homesteads from John's property. In less than ten years, this adventurous hard working man went from living in a palmetto hut with harden clay floor to a very prosperous businessman owning two large two-story houses, multiple sailing skiffs, and had several men working for him. When he lost almost everything in the storm of 1909, he not only survived the disaster, but he overcame it and sprang back to his feet. Resettling on higher ground along Bayou Petit Caillou, he focused his skills on building larger boats.

When relatives went to visit John's family, they would always note that he rarely took time off from work. He was known for working from before the sunrise till long past the sunset. I cannot tell the exact number of the boats my great-grandfather built himself, but from interviews I did with the first-hand witnesses I would estimate somewhere around several dozens, most of them being smaller skiffs with that last one being around 1943. Once John's wife had a stroke in the early 1940's, he never took up building boats again. In addition to his boat building heritage, John [A. b: 1874; 8-II] had left a saying reminding us of him every time someone uses it: "With a hammer and nail, I can build the world". An interesting side note, all of his daughters averaged around 4' 10" and his sons were around 5' 4" tall.

In the mid-1960s, Lee Roy J. Pitre, Sr. [A.b.1928; 10-III] had two more sons with Anna Lou Theriot. They were Jarvis John Pitre [b.1964; 11-III] and Eric Daniel Pitre [b.1965; 11-IV].

1970s

Beginning with 1972, the further career of my father was connected with the Dwight Andrus Homes where he was working as Shop Foreman for cabinet department of their home manufacturing division for many years. He was making $13.5 K per year. This job brought him the recognition of the master in cabinetry throughout the Southeastern states and gave a good start for his middle son's own business. Lee Roy, Sr. (b.1928; 10-III) was still occasionally building the boats as the opportunity for additional money on the side.

As I already mentioned, sometime in 1972, Wilbert Pitre [b.1923; 10-I], Lee Roy, Sr.'s older brother, was able to buy out Quentin Cunningham's share of the boat company. On September 20, 1972, he registered Pitre Shipyard, Inc. with the state.

The year of 1972 brought some good changes. Lee Roy, Sr. [A.b.1928; 10-III] saved enough money to purchase a little over an acre of land just southwest of the Lafayette city limits. There were some other exciting changes for the family at that summer. For it was that time, when I began my first paying job. Lee Roy, Jr. [b.1960; 11-II], that is I – your humble author – was hired on as a carpenter apprentice to work alongside with my father during the summers and school holidays. Although I started with a small payment of $1 per hour, and it was hard work in the hot shop for about 50 hours a week, I was eager to learn. Throughout the next three summers, I worked under a guidance of numerous skilled construction workers learning many concepts of home building. In summer of 1974, Lee Roy, Sr. [A.b.1928; 10-III] and Anna Lou (A.b.1928) sold their old house on the north side and moved to their property on Huggins Road just off Guilbeau Road (now it is known as West Congress Street). With the help of his wife and three sons, Lee Roy, Sr. developed the land and maintained a large garden where they had various fruit trees, pecans, and vegetables bringing some additional income to the family.

In 1975 Lee Roy, Sr.'s income rose to $15.2 K per year. He was still with the Dwight Andrus Homes. The salary definitely was not a fair compensation for a quality and hard work, but it was enough to cover the bills and necessities for his family.

Even though Élie Joseph Pitre [A.b.1898; 9-II] was a cancer survivor, he finally succumbed to a massive heart attack and died on June 24, 1978 at the age of 80. He was buried alongside of his father John Lee Pitre [A.b.1874; 8-II] on the cemetery's front row next to St. Joseph's Catholic Church in Chauvin, Louisiana. He was married four times and outlived all four of his wives. Rumor has it there was a fifth wife, but I was unable to confirm it.

In 1980, Lee Roy, Sr. (A.b.1928; 10-III) was working as cabinet department shop foreman for $23.2K per year. In the mid-1980s, when the decision to shut down the home manufacturing division of Dwight Andrus Homes was made by the ownership, Lee Roy (A.b.1928; 10-III) maintained his livelihood by continuing to do odd carpentry jobs as people in the area came to him with personal requests for furniture or other household items made of wood. By his 60th birthday in 1988, he found himself pretty much fully retired and enjoying life as he knew it.

During 1984, the people of South Central Louisiana saw the end of another era, when Wisteria (b.1897; 9-I) passed away on June 26. She was a very eccentric person, but her life made a huge impact on people along Bayou Terrebonne and Petit Caillou.

THE 21ST CENTURY

The 21st century brought on some of the worst fears of the Americans and people worldwide along with many breakthrough in science, technology, and modern medicine. George Walker Bush was sworn in as the 43rd President of the United States in 2001 and led the country into a war which was unlike any other war we experienced.

On September 11, 2001, the lives of everyone were changed forever. An Islamic terrorist group known as Al-Qaeda successfully launched a series of coordinated attacks against the people of the United States in their war against all western cultures. Approximately 3,000 people lost their lives when four hijacked planes were intentionally crashed into the Twin towers, the Pentagon, and a field in Pennsylvania.

In 2005, still in the middle of his war on terrorism, George Walker Bush began the second term as the President of the United States. As if fighting an unconventional global war against terrorism was not enough, in the fall of 2005, the United States Gulf Coast suffered two of the most intense storms in recorded history—Katrina and Rita.

Although hurricane Katrina had weakened to a category 3 storm by the time it hit southeast Louisiana on August 29, 2005, it had grown to immense size. When levies in New Orleans were overtopped by the incoming waves of Lake Pontchartrain and failed, the unthinkable happened, and New Orleans began to flood. The Mississippi and Alabama gulf coast took the blunt of the surge estimated to be 27 feet high in some areas. Mother Nature was not yet done dumping her wrath on the Gulf Coast. On September 24, just one month later, another hurricane – Rita – made a landfall between Sabine Pass and Johnson Bayou. It was also a category 3 storm when it reached the coast. At the time, Hurricane Rita was considered the fourth, most intense Atlantic storm as well as the most forceful ever observed in the Gulf of Mexico. Its surge and destructive winds caused widespread damage along most of the Louisiana coastline. In some cases, the storm destroyed entire coastal communities without a single building left standing.

In the small town of Delcambre, Louisiana, with nowhere for the slow waters of Bayou Carlin to go, the enormous surge coming through the Vermillion bay forced the bayou to rise quickly. Residents had just a few minutes to grab what they could and evacuate north of Highway 14 and the railroad. Although Delcambre like many other south central Louisiana towns encountered hurricanes before, people were not ready to what happened during Rita. Never in recorded history had the water raised that high before so quickly. Most homes south of Louisiana Highway 14 had water up to the roof tops. Wilbert [(b.1923; 10-I)] and Hilda Pitre lost practically everything that was in their home.

Still living in a FEMA trailer while waiting for their home to be elevated and rebuilt, Wilbert [(b.1923; 10-I)] Pitre died on March 30, 2006. His wife, Hilda outlived her husband for 11 months and passed away on March 2, 2007. Together during their 65 years of marriage, Wilbert and Hilda had two sons, six grandchildren, and six great-grandchildren.

Meanwhile, Lee Roy, Sr. [(A.b.1928; 10-III)] spent the beginning of the 21st century enjoying a quiet and modest retirement. Occasionally he would take on a carpentry job, but preferred spending his time visiting relatives, friends and telling stories of the days long gone by. As he reached the later part of his life, Lee Roy Sr. communicated his some last wishes before he died. First, that each of his sons would be married and have children of their own, and second, that he would be retired and be able to "burn at least 10 years of social security." Both of his wishes eventually came to be true.

With his passing, 2006 marked the closing of another chapter in the life and times of the Pitres. Lee Roy J. Pitre, Sr. [(A.b.1928; 10-III)] passed away of natural causes on October 14, 2006, in Lafayette, Louisiana. He left behind one daughter, three sons, 12 grandchildren, and seven great-grandkids who would continue the Pitre line. There will be many more chapters yet to come and more stories to tell.

Although, Lee Roy, Sr. [(A.b.1928; 10-III)] often wished he had stayed in school early in life as well as staying in the National Guard till retirement, he lived a quite comfortable but modest life. Occasionally, he talked about his dream of becoming an archeologist if he had stayed in school. Having completed only seven grades of public education from the small school house along Bayou Little Caillou, he had enough intelligence, patience, and strict financial rules that allowed him to acquire 1.3 acres of land. He and his family never went hungry and had no debts upon his passing. Many in south Louisiana will remember Lee Roy, Sr. for his mastery of carpentry skills in many fine homes. However, to some of us, he will be recognized and remembered because of who and what we have become in life. Without him and all of our ancestors and what they strived to overcome in life, we would not be here today.

The branch of the Pitre heritage that I am a member of is only one of many across North America and is now in its 13th generation from Jean Pitre [(A.b.1635)] and Marie Pesseley, including not only South Central Louisiana but North Texas. With continued perseverance, the Pitre family line will carry on to enlarge and prosper for many generations to come.

NON-ACADIAN FAMILIES in LOUISIANA

The great majority, if not all, of the Pitres of South Louisiana are descendants of Jean Pitre, the edge toolmaker from Flanders and Port Royal. However, a Spanish family named Pitre lived in New Orleans during the late colonial period. One may wonder if they were the ancestors of the Pitres counted in New Orleans and Barataria in Jefferson Parish, south of the city, in 1850 (the Barataria Pitres could very well have been Acadians who migrated east from the lower Lafourche valley). After the War Between the States, freed persons named Pitre, probably former slaves owned by members of the family, lived in St. Landry Parish.

The family's name also is spelled Pierre, Pike, Pite, Pittre, Spitre, and Pitre. Members of the family on the western prairies favor the pronunciation [PEET], but their cousins on the southeastern bayous tend to call themselves [PEE-tree].

The great majority of the Pitres of South Louisiana are Acadians, but a German called Pitre lived at New Orleans in the late 1720s. There was also a Pitre from Spain who lived in the city during the late colonial period, while another Pitre from Arkansas may have settled in Louisiana during the Antebellum Period.

Pierre, called Pitre, a "German, native of St. Angile," son of Michel Rose and Marianne Rose, died at New Orleans in September 1727. The priest who recorded his burial did not give Pierre/Pitre's age at the time of his death or mention his wife.

Antonio Pitre of San Juan del Hoyo, Galicia, Spain, married Josefa Salazar, a native of New Orleans, probably in the 1790s. Their son Manuel was born in New Orleans in October, 1802 but died in November.

Marie, daughter of Pierre Pitre and Hélène Embeau of Arkansas Territory, married Daniel, son of François Coussot of Arkansas, probably at Arkansas Post in July, 1834. The former French colony of Arkansas became a United States territory in 1819 and a state of the Union in June, 1836. Was Marie's father an Acadian Pitre whose parents had found refuge in Canada during Le Grand Dérangement? That is still a question.

Other Louisiana Branches

      Pierre Pitre was one of the earliest Acadians who took refuge in Louisiana[40]. A widower along with his two children, Catherine, 22, and Francois, 17, they reached New Orleans from Halifax around 1765. They were included in a small number of Acadians who were sent to the Opelousas District in present day St. Landry Parish. They settled around Pleasance and Grand Prairie. Few of his descendants married other Acadians. His daughter married French Creole Pierre Joubert during 1760s. Some eventually moved westward to Eunice and Ville Platte which is now part of Evangeline Parish. Others decided to move southward near Church Point along the Bayou Plaquemine Brule.

      Over fifty Pitres came to the colony from the mother country aboard five of the Seven Ships in 1785. Interestingly, none of them joined their cousins on the Opelousas prairies. They settled, instead, on upper Bayou LaFourche and north of Baton Rouge. By the early Antebellum Period, the Pitre families disappeared from the river and did not return, at least, any of them before the War Between the States. Meanwhile, the Lafourche/Terrebonne valley emerged as a major center of the Pitre family settlement. Most of the Pitres of Ascension and Assumption parishes moved down bayou into Lafourche Interior and Terrebonne parishes, where they settled near Thibodaux, Raceland, Lockport, Larose, Golden Meadow, Houma, and Montegut. A family from Bayou LaFourche moved to lower Bayou Teche in the 1840s, but the great majority of their cousins remained on the southeastern bayous and at the edge of the Lafourche and Terrebonne marshes.

Isle Aú Pitre

Isle Aú Pitre was originally known as Isle Aú Pied meaning Island of Tracks. It was renamed sometime after 1851 but before 1902. According to a post by Richard Ruttley, Jr., he claim through family stories, the Island was named after Alonzo Mack Pitre birth unknown. He died in New Orleans and was married to Josephine St. Amant. They had one son, whom they named Charles Alonzo Pitre.

Antonio Domigo Pitre b. 1778 Aan Julian deLoyra, Galica, Spain; d. 12/12/1841, New Orleans.
Dominique "Domingo" Mathieu Charles Pitre, b. 03/14/1819, New Orleans.
Domingo P. Pitre, b.1838, New Orleans, Carpenter.
Alonzo M. Pitre, b. 1871, Occupation Swamp railroad ties.
Charles Alonzo Pitre, d. Marrero, Jefferson parish
Per Richard Ruttley, Jr. Isle Au Pitre was named after his grandfather's family.

Isle of the Chitamachas

Initially "Isle of the Chitamachas" was settled by Indians. In 1763 Monsieur Du Rollin was given a land grant to the Cheniere which was later sold to Francisco Caminada who gave its current name. It is also known as "Chico Isle", "Chita", "Caminadaville", and "Grand Chénière" – meaning "great oak ridge."

---

[40] … http://www.acadiansingray.com/

Annapolis Valley Trip

I had been planning to make a research trip to Nova Scotia for several years. Each time things happened and I had to delay my plans. However, around mid-March of 2013, I decided it was time to stop making excuses and go there since it is a critical part of research for my book. As I was preparing for a trip, Annette Hebert-Autio contacted me on March 23 indicating she wanted to possibly meet in Nova Scotia. Annette is a retired school teacher who lives in Edmonton, Alberta, towards central Canada. Her daughter, Jacquie Lindquist lives in Toronto, Ontario, just northwest of New York. So the mother and daughter made plans for Annette to fly over to Jacquie, meet in Toronto, and then Jacquie would drive over to Annapolis Royal and meet with me.

Annette is my distant relative and her ancestral lineage traces back to Jean [A.b.1636], Marc [b.1674], Jean-Baptiste [b.1703], and Jean Pitre [b.1732].

Annette also informed me about her second cousin, Marcel Ralph Pitre from Pine Falls, Manitoba. Marcel is a writer and chronicler of family stories. He is an enthusiastic historian and genealogist who wrote a book about his ancestors around 2010. In his turn, Marcel put Annette in touch with another cousin, Fernand Pitre from Nova Scotia. Fernand "Fern" is a retired engineer and also owns a cottage on the southern bank of Annapolis River in Clementsport located southwest of Goat Island. As it became evident, a few years earlier, Fern had the opportunity to purchase the undeveloped land that Claude Pitre owned in 1707. He wanted to acquire the property and ensure it remained undeveloped and in the hands of the Pitres. Upon, finding out about this, I could not miss a chance to stand upon an early 18th century Pitre homestead. Therefore, I made my final travel arrangements and planned on spending July 21 through 27 of 2013 along the Annapolis Valley.

When Fern heard about Annette's and my trip, he generously offered to schedule a meet-and-greet dinner at his cottage in Clementsport. In the conversation before the dinner, Fern mentioned about a famous Acadian historian living across the highway from Fern's cottage and said that he would try to invite that person over for the dinner. This historian is none other than Wayne Melanson who is the interpretation officer, coordinator, and tour guide for the Port Royal National Historic Habitation site.

I flew into the Halifax airport on July 21st and picked up my rental car. Since my flight did not arrive in Halifax until after midnight, I was thinking about getting a motel to sleep a few hours. However, I was way too excited to sleep knowing I was only a few hours away from the 17th century land of my ancestors. So I decided to hit the road and headed towards Annapolis Royal.

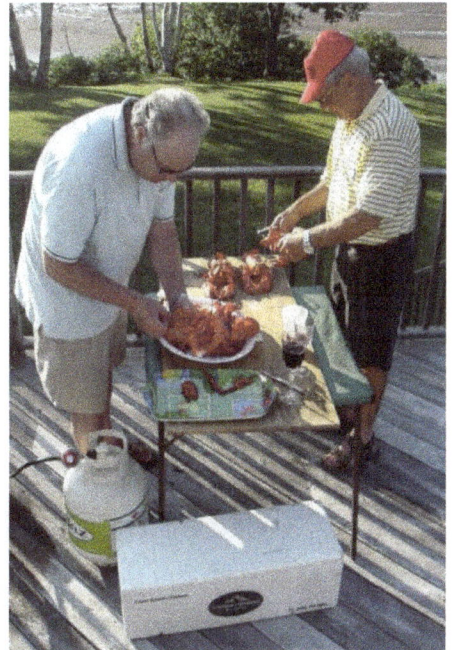

Figure 43 : Sidney Burrel & Fern Pitre preparing our feast

As I made my way through the country side and reached the Annapolis Valley, I could not help myself of thinking back to the 17th and 18th centuries and wondering what life was really like for my first ancestors in North America.

I wanted to make maximum use of my limited research time in Annapolis Royal, so I had made reservations at the Turret Bed & Breakfast, which was within walking distance from most of the major historic sites in downtown. However, check in was not until 10a.m. Therefore, I decided to link up with Annette and Jacquie at the house they rented in Parker's Cove. I arrived there early and truly enjoyed watching the sun rise across the Bay of Fundy. As I sat there on the edge of the bank waiting for Annette and Jacquie to wake, I found myself reminiscing about one class lesson so many years ago. It was about the extreme high and low tides in the Bay of Fundy. Back then I never realized some of my ancestors made their homesteads along this valley, but often thought I could visit the place one day. And, yet, here I was. Later that morning, we synced up our various schedules for the week. Fern was going to meet us Tuesday afternoon at the house Annette and Jacquie were renting. That gave me a couple of days to explore downtown.

On Tuesday afternoon, Fern showed up as promised to lead us to his cottage in Clementsport for dinner. There came several people that I did not know. It was a very gracious and enjoyable social. Except for the local cuisine and slightly different dialect, the hospitality and atmosphere was very similar to Cajuns in south Louisiana. There I met Wayne Melanson, a historian Fern invited, and we spent quite a bit of time talking about L'Acadie. His knowledge and ability to speak about historical events in detail hour after hour was quite impressive. Meanwhile Fern prepared a feast of lobsters which were truly tasty.

Figure 44 : Wayne Melanson

On Wednesday morning, Fern again met up with us to tour Claude's 18th century homestead further up the Annapolis Valley. As I walked through the Pitre's homestead, saw the stone fence lines, stone basement ruins, water well, and the remains of the stone foundation for the windmill, my passion for more information turned into an obsession. I was like a little kid who entered a candy store for the first time.

Next day, on Thursday night, I met with Alan Melanson, Wayne's twin brother, for the midnight Acadian Graveyard tour. I also spent most of the next day with Wayne at the Port Royal Habitation. I must admit, of all of my travels and tours, these two were about the most enjoyable and informative I have ever experienced.

Figure 45 : Fernand Pitre & Lee Roy Pitre, Claude Pitre homestead c.1710

On my return trip to Halifax, I stopped and spent several hours exploring the Acadian museum at Grand Pre as well as the exportation site. Unfortunately, my first trip to Nova Scotia was too short, and I did not have enough time to visit the historical sites in Île Saint Jean, known as Prince Edward Island today. I eagerly look forward to my next visit to Nova Scotia and plan on spending more time there breathing in a strong spirit of my ancestors.

Figure 46 : Alan and Durline Melanson

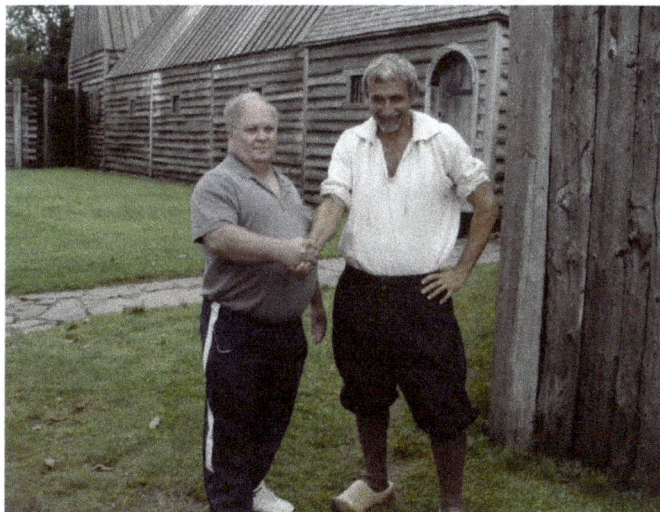

Figure 47 : Lee Roy Pitre (left) Wayne Melanson (right)

Figure 48 : Acadian Graves - Mid 17th Century

Saint - Jean - Baptiste
Parish Cemetery
(c.1632 - 1755)
"Well before this became the British garrison graveyard in 1710, it was the Saint-Jean Baptiste parish cemetery and was used by the Acadian community of Port Royal and by the French garrison."

Figure 49 : Annapolis River low tide

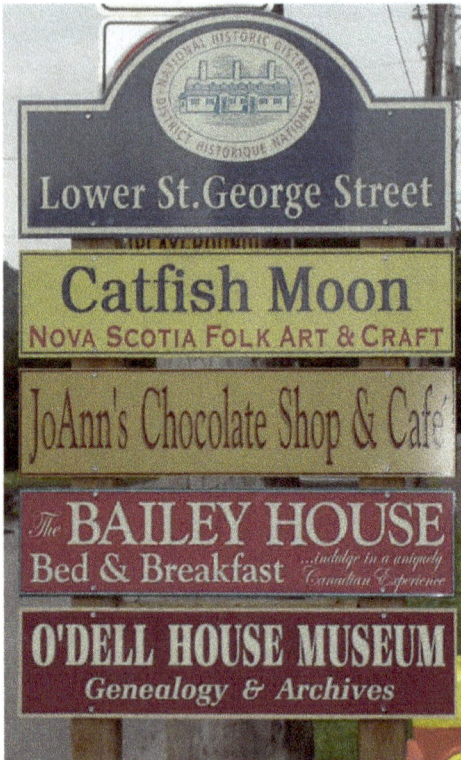

Lower St.George Street

Catfish Moon
NOVA SCOTIA FOLK ART & CRAFT

JoAnn's Chocolate Shop & Café

The BAILEY HOUSE
Bed & Breakfast ...Indulge in a uniquely Canadian Experience

O'DELL HOUSE MUSEUM
Genealogy & Archives

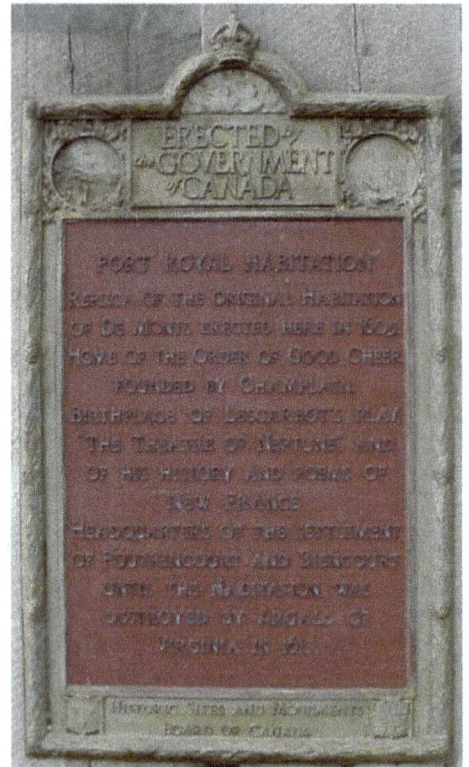

ERECTED
BY GOVERNMENT
OF CANADA

PORT ROYAL HABITATION
REPLICA OF THE ORIGINAL HABITATION
OF DE MONTS ERECTED HERE IN 1605

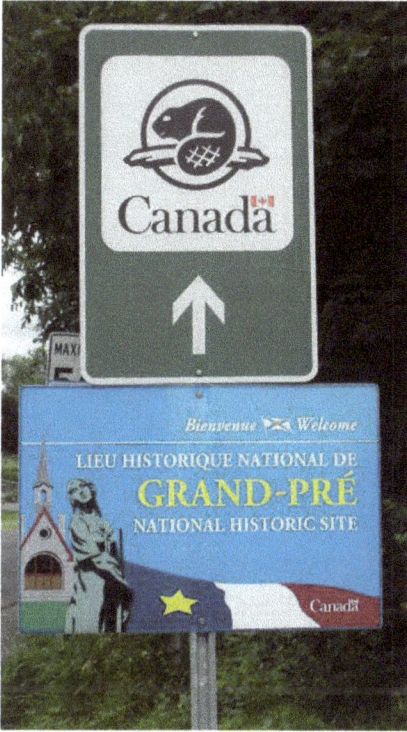

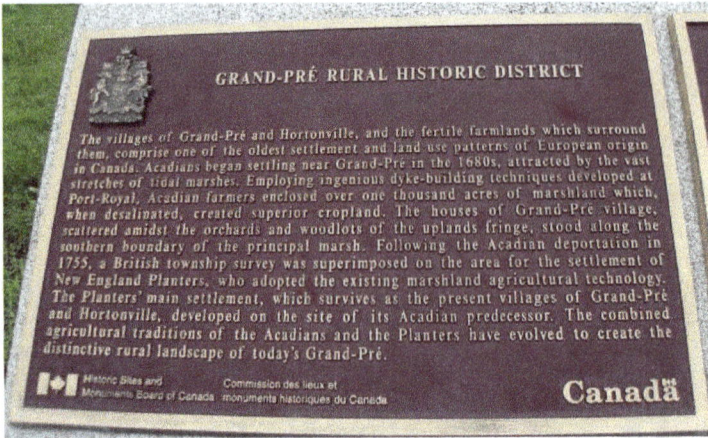

GRAND-PRÉ RURAL HISTORIC DISTRICT

The villages of Grand-Pré and Hortonville, and the fertile farmlands which surround them, comprise one of the oldest settlement and land use patterns of European origin in Canada. Acadians began settling near Grand-Pré in the 1680s, attracted by the vast stretches of tidal marshes. Employing ingenious dyke-building techniques developed at Port-Royal, Acadian farmers enclosed over one thousand acres of marshland which, when desalinated, created superior cropland. The houses of Grand-Pré village, scattered amidst the orchards and woodlots of the uplands fringe, stood along the southern boundary of the principal marsh. Following the Acadian deportation in 1755, a British township survey was superimposed on the area for the settlement of New England Planters, who adopted the existing marshland agricultural technology. The Planters' main settlement, which survives as the present villages of Grand-Pré and Hortonville, developed on the site of its Acadian predecessor. The combined agricultural traditions of the Acadians and the Planters have evolved to create the distinctive rural landscape of today's Grand-Pré.

Historic Sites and Monuments Board of Canada   Commission des lieux et monuments historiques du Canada   **Canadä**

Theories of Jean Pitre's Origin

If one explores various genealogy sites deep enough, he or she can find that Jean's [(A.b:1636; I)] parents are either *Mathurian Pitre* and *Felicite Thibodeau* or *Simon Pitre* and *Marie Louise Mezey*. However, I have contacted most of the website administrators, and none were able to provide any authentic documents to support that claim. Most of them admitted to have copied the names from someone else's post. Historians believe they are simply replicating errors someone made many years earlier.

Internationally renowned, Professor Stephen White cites in his *Dictionaire Généalogique des Familles Acadiennes*, that Farther Clarence d'Entremont believed it was more likely Jean [(A.b:1636; I)] was of English descent or at least lived in England prior to moving to Port Royal. He based this on accounts of Customs and Manners of the Micmakis and Maricheets. Father Clarence d'Entremont[41] speculated that *Jean Pitre* [(b: 1636; I)] might have changed his name from Peters. He also stated there was an account of a blacksmith by the name of John Peters coming over from England. Many other publications stated that *Jean* [(A.b:1636; I)] most likely changed his name from either Peters, Pietr, Pieter, or Pitran for various reasons.

Many people in their books and various web sites have cited the book titled *History of Saint Anthony Parish 1803 – 1980* as the definitive source document that *Jan Pietres* is one in the same as *Jean Pitre* (circa 1636 - 1689).

If one consults a copy of the book and refer to page 148 under the section titled *Descendants of Ebenezer Peters Who Settled in Fortune Cove in 1870*, it states that

> …Jan Pietres who came to Acadia in 1658 from the settlement of Permambuco, Brazil.

> … In 1664, Jan married Marie Pesselin and they settled in Beaubassin, now Amherst.

Further, the author claims that Jan's son and grandson married Francoise Babin and Marguerite Terriot. One must be very careful about making this kind of statements. Just like today, there were numerous people living in mid-17th century L'Acadie that had the same first and last names. The last statement of relevance in the section I am analyzing here explains that the more easily pronounced name "Peters" was used by some and that other descendants used the name "Pitre".

---

[41] Farther Clarence d'Entremont, Histoire du Cap-Sable [Eunice, Louisiana: Hébert Publications, 1981], Vol. III, p. 1050

However, unless I missed it, nowhere do these pages mention the name "Jean Pitre" or draw any type of conclusion connecting these two men as the same one.

Based on detailed analysis of many years of painstaking research, all of these theories and others appear to be a long stretch. They do not seem plausible taking into account the times and places. On the other hand, who am I to make such bold statements in opposition to other historical researchers? My only strong point is that I attempt to support each of my claims with original recorded documents.

Although, it is possible it may exist, I have not found any hard documentation in its original source dating back to 1658, stating that a Jan Pietres arrived in Port Royal. If one was to assume that a Jan Pietres did in fact exist and settled in Beaubassin by way of Port Royal, careful analysis of known facts, one would have to reason that these were two different men.

The first known census of L'Acadie was conducted in 1671[42]. Beaubassin was initially settled in 1672, after the 1671 census. Therefore, it was not included in that census. It listed "*Jean Pitre*," age 35, married circa 1664 to "*Marie Peselet*," age 26, as living between "*Pierre Commeaux*," age 75, and "*Etienne Commeaux*," age 2,1 among the "Port Royal" area residents. An important note here is that the settlement along the Riviere du Dauphin (present day Annapolis Valley) is a great distance from the Beaubassin settlement of 1672.

In Jean's [(A.b:1636; I)] own account in the census of 1671, he stated that his profession at the time was a "taillandier." It is generally understood that taillandier in the mid-1600s closely translates to meaning "tool maker". Although both trades deal with metal, there is a clear difference between a blacksmith and taillandier. Moreover, by 1678, Jean had acquired two acres of land that he had under cultivation up the river from Port Royal where he was living at the time. A blacksmith would surely be more prosperous living in or on the outskirts of Port Royal as opposed to cultivating several miles up Riviere du Dauphin.

---

[42] 1671 Census, MIKAN no. 2319362, http://collectionscanada.gc.ca/pam_archives/index.php?fuseaction=genitem.displayItem&rec_nbr=2319362

The Journey Thus Far

Concluding this book does not mean the journey is over. It is still an ongoing exploration of the past. Some of the same questions persist: Who were Jean Pitre's [A.b:1636; I] parents? Where was he born? What was the ethnic make-up of his bloodline? Where were his parents born? Who were his grandparents? Why and how did he end up in North America? The more information I collect, the more questions keep arising.

I definitely agree with Professor Stephen White and others, that with the absence of any hard documents containing traces of Jean's [A.b:1636; I] lineage, such as his birth, baptismal, or marriage certificate, we may never be able to definitely answer any lingering questions, historically speaking.

Scientifically, it may be a different issue. As the science of DNA analysis evolves, maybe with advanced Information Technology methodologies, a database of paternal DNA of male Pitre descendants, may yet yield conclusive information as to fifteenth century and ancient Pitre paternal ethnic blood lines. I did submit my DNA for such studies. Unfortunately, the results have not been processed in time for the first printing of my book. I will include it in a revised copy.

Due to the nature of events, culture and lifestyles during the middle ages and following centuries, the answers to these questions may be lost to history. As I explained in the beginning of this book, only information about the descendants of nobility and landowners during the Middle Ages in Europe was well documented. The common people were too busy surviving day to day challenges of life and had little to no time to worry about proper recording of their ancestors and descendants.

I am still pondering over the same questions. Why would the average commoner move from mid-seventeenth century Europe to North America? Was it primarily due to persecution of Huguenots or simply pursuit of adventure or more prosperous life? We may never know for sure since each person's journey through life has its own story of circumstances, hardships, opportunities, and other events. However, careful and detailed analysis of what history has recorded of the times may have left us some clues.

I believe that my theories are more than coincidental. It is with certainty I draw my paternal ancestral bloodline directly back to the regions of Normandy and Southern Belgium in Europe. Jean Pitre's [A.b:1636; I] parents were most likely the descendants of traveling merchants that eventually settled in the country of Flanders. Moreover, I am convinced that my 16th century ancestors were from the *Villa de Pîtres.* They took on the family surname of *Pître* sometime during the mid-Middle

Ages, thus indicating the geographical region they were from as presented in my prologue. Since there is no direct evidence of my ancestors being of noble birth, the Pitre coat of Arms does not apply to my ancestors. Coat of Arms was a sign of nobility and title of an "individual" and not something passed down to all family members.

However, what was the ethnic origin of Jean Pitre's [(A.b:1636; I)] paternal ancestors? It is plausible, that his ancestors are a mixture of Dutch, Normans, Gauls, Scandinavian, and Francs. Based on my research analysis, I will go on a limb and state that I firmly believe he was mostly Dutch with perhaps some mixture of Norman, Gaul's, and maybe even Scandinavian. I doubt he was a descendant of any Francs, although I could be wrong. It seems that European migrations, occurring prior to the 17th century, were going more westward than to the east. The exception might involve traveling merchants who have decided to settle in the northeast later. Perhaps, as the science of heredity research through DNA analysis matures more for paternal lineage and enough of Jean's [(A.b:1636; I)] descendants take the test, we will eventually have sufficient facts to determine his ethnic blood line.

According to one of Jean's [(A.b:1636; I)] grandsons, Claude Marc Pitre [(b.1700; 3-I)], Jean [(A.b:1636; I)] was of Flemish origin. His declaration on February 28, 1767, after resettling in Bell Ile en Mer[43] was rather simple and based on his understanding of what he was told by his ancestors. Historically, the word "Flemish" refers to the name of the language of the western region of the former country of Flanders and not necessarily the makeup of one's ethnic bloodline. Prior to Flanders split into lower Belgium and northern France, there were four main Dutch dialects consisting of Barbantian, East Flemish, West Flemish, and Limburgish. So was Claude indicating the region his ancestors were born or their ethnic bloodline? Any statement or translation about such would be purely speculation without hard documentation or further scientific evidence.

Many people may believe that Cajuns descend solely from Acadians exiled from Nova Scotia, who eventually settled in South Louisiana during the 18th and 19th centuries. Others think they are descendants of French. One of the biggest discoveries I made throughout my journey is that it is not so simple, just like many things in life. Upon deeper analysis of the various 15th and 16th century families that lived in Nova Scotia and Prince Edward Island, it strictly depends on who the ancestors were. Many of them were descendants of not only French, but that of Scotts, Dutch, German, and Scandinavian. Many also descend from other ethnic groups, whom they intermarried with over many generations, including English, Spanish, German, French, Creole, and others.

---

[43] The Acadians in France, Vol. 2, Belle Isle en Mer Registers, Milton P. Rieder, Jr. and Norma Gaudet Rieder

What I do know, just like so many Cajuns and Louisiana settlers, that the Pitres living in Louisiana, seem to be mostly of Acadian descendant. However, my journey has revealed traces of French, Italian, Spanish, English, German, and possibly Scandinavian roots on the maternal side of my ancestors. I continue researching and plowing deeper some of the details, and I intend including the results in the second edition of my book.

Some people believe that the Pitre's of Louisiana are descendants of the two Pitre brothers that landed in south Louisiana. They say these brothers were descendants of a long line of ship builders and they paid off their trans-Atlantic voyage by doing odd jobs on various ships and schooners. This did not prove to be an accurate claim. As I have detailed throughout this book, all Pitre's that arrived in Louisiana are well documented regarding to ship they arrived on and where they debarked. There were actually multiple Pitre families that immigrated to Louisiana; the vast majority of them were descendants of Jean Denis Pitre [A.b.1680; 2-VII]. In Louisiana, they settled mainly around Opelousas, Ville Platte, Terrebonne, and Lafourche. However, they spread out over the years nationwide with bulk remaining in South Louisiana.

Although, I have not suffered as much as people of other cultures and ethnic races, my journey through life and that of my ancestors was difficult. Life challenges taught me some valuable lessons.

Today more than ever, hate drives many individuals and cultures. Many of them are blaming others for their perceived status in life. I also feel like blaming the English and French of the past for discrimination and expulsion of my ancestors. However, one huge lesson I have learned from this journey back in time is that I am here experiencing what life has to offer because of the path of my ancestors. Any slight deviation and I simply may never have existed.

Instead of everyone wrongly accusing others for what went wrong in their lives and of their ancestors, they should be thankful for the blessings that have been dealt to them. Life as we know it is not some magical thing. The meaning of life is rather simple: to experience the simple pleasures of a physical existence and to pass on that knowledge. What I have and who I am are determined by the DNA gift passed on to me by my parents and my God given free will. Everyone has the same, and it is up to us what we make of our lives.

It reminded me of many of the hard times and controversies of today and some people's desire for reparations to compensate the suffering, challenges, and struggles of their ancestors. I, however, formed a very different perspective during the process of connecting the dots uncovered during my journey. In no way am I condoning or defending oppressors or violators of human rights. I do though realize that the only reason I am alive today is because of direct and indirect results of each and every event whether it was good or bad.

If my grandfather had not taken the risk of moving from Chauvin to create a partnership with Cunningham, my father would not have met my mother.

If not for the hurricanes of 1909 and 1926, my great grandfather (John Lee (A.b:1876; 8-II) Pitre) would not have moved from lower Bayou LaCache to lower Montegut and then Chauvin, thus minimizing the chances of my grandfather meeting and marrying my grandmother.

If not for the Civil War, my great great-grandfather would most likely not moved from Chénière Caminada to Raceland, therefore minimizing the possibility of him meeting and marrying my great great-grandmother down lower Bayou LaCache.

If not for the Spanish commission of invitation to the exiled Acadians in France to help settle Louisiana, the odds that my third and fourth great-grandfathers of meeting and marrying my third and fourth great-grandmothers. As a result, my fifth great grandmother would not have immigrated to Louisiana in 1785 aboard the ship *L'Amite*.

If not for Le Grand Derangement, in which the English expulsed the French from Acadia during 1755 through 1759, my fifth great-grandfather's first wife would not have died at sea during their expulsion trip from Île Royal in Acadia. Thus, he would not have married my fifth great-grandmother during their exile in France.

Because of the repeated aggression by the English during the 1600s and early 1700s, my third, fourth, and fifth great-grandfathers might not have been born, since my second and eventually third great-grandfather would probably not have continued to elude the English by going further north.

If any of those events and many others had not happened, it would have been astronomically improbable for me to be privileged with the experiences of life and become the person I am today. Many of my ancestors and I would never have been born.

So instead of focusing on blaming and expecting others for the suffering and injustices of my ancestors or expecting reparations for their suffering, I cherish the good things in life that I have inherited from them, including culture, traditions, blood line. I never forget the important lessons learned centering my concerns more on the *here* and *now* and *how* I can improve this life and future.

I have a significant amount of additional research that I chose not to include in my first book, simply because I have spent many years researching, and it still seems to be in the progress. Due to many delays, both personal and professional, the publication was postponed several times. I realized that I needed to draw a line, place a period at some point, and publish my book with everything I have collected and analyzed so far before I myself become a whisper in the wind of yesteryears. Therefore, it is my intention to publish a second edition later as I gather more evidence and documents to advance my research.

I am in communication with several historians and historical societies concerning the ancient lands and times of my ancestors. It is also my intent to make additional trips to these various lands of my ancestors during the next few years if my health and finances are yield the feasibility of such distant trips.

Some myths and folklore were discussed, many interesting and historical facts uncovered. In addition, some surprising lessons were learned along the way. This book's research agenda allowed me to discover many details around the historical events in connection with my ancestors.

Some of the significant events, both positive and negative, brought major disruptions to their lives. Nevertheless, our ancestors were of a very hearty and creative stock with a proud sense of rich culture as their heritage and legacy. They kept their heritage and traditions alive throughout turbulent and hardship times.

It means the Pitres will go on across the states, countries, and even continents for many-many centuries in the future. And as long as they will, the journey will continue, just as life always finds a way to thrive against the odds.

My Family Tree

Jean (Jehan) Pitre b: Abt. 1636 "d'origine flamande"; d: Abt 1689 Port Royal, Acadia									
Marie Pesseley b: Abt 1645 Port Royal; m: Abt 1665 Port Royal [Isaac Pesseley/Barbe Bajolet]; d: 12/26/1707 Port Royal									
2	**Jean Denis Pitre II** b: Abt 1680 Port Royal; d: Aft 1724, laborer & sales flour mill belonging to step farther								
VII	**Francoise Babin** b: Abt 1681 Port Royal; m: Abt 1698 Port Royal; D: aFT 1724 [Antoine/Marie Mercier]								
	3	**Claude Jean Pitre** b:1701 Acadia; d: bef 10/27/1759 - ?????							
	III	**Marguerite Doiron** b: Abt 1708 Acadia; m: 1724; d: Bef 10/27/1759 [Noel/Marie Henry]							
		4	**Benjamin Pitre** b: 1725 Cobequit Acadia; d: 9/30/1782 St Pierre de Reze, Bretagne, France - ????						
		I	**Marie Marguerite Boudreaux** (Boudrot) b: abt 1740 Acadia; m: 11/27/1759; d: Aft 1799 Louisiana [Jean Baptiste/Catherine Brassard]						
			5	**Jean Baptiste Francois Pitre** b: 8/12/1773 or 10/2/1780 St Pierre de Reze, Bretagne France; d: Bet 1813/1832 Ascension, LA					
			XII	**Marie Anne Reine Bourg** b: 11/17/1787 Donaldsonville, LA; m: 9/1/1808; d: 11/10/1832 Thibodaux [Jean/Catherine Viaud]					
				6	**Jean Florentine Pitre II** b: 3/31/1811 Plattenville, Louisiana; d: 10/27/1886 Thibodaux, Louisiana - Farmer				
				I	**Susanne Zulma (Toups)** b: 10/8/1816 Plattenville, Assumption; m: 8/31/1840; d: Abt 1/25/1898 [Drausin Toups]				
					7	**Elie Pierre Pitre** b: 8/26/1841 Lafourche; d: 9/19/1898 Terrebonne, Louisiana - Farmer			
					I	**Mathilda Cornelia White** b: 10/7/1850 Houma; m: 9/13/1873 Montegut; D: 4/29/1934 Montegut [Daniel William/Eliza Pierce]			
						8	**John Elie Pitre** b: June or July 2/1874 Montegut; d: 8/4/1965 Chauvin - House Carpenter		
						II	**Marie Frances Autin** b: 3/29/1879; m: 5/5/1896 Houma; d: 12/4/1953 [Charles Henry Autin / Eliza Louise Viteaux]		
							9	**Elie Joseph Pitre** b: 2/8/1898 Montegut; d: 6/24/1978 Delcambre - Carpenter specializing in Shrimp Boats	
							II	**Leona A. (LeBouef)** b: 1/30/1900 Terrebonne; m: Abt 1921; d: 8/15/1934 [Battie LeBouef / Olamp]	
								10	**Wilbert Pitre** b: 3/7/1923; d: 3/30/2006 Delcambre - Owner/President Pitre Ship Yard - specializing in Shrimp Boats
								I	**Hilda (Boudloche) Pitre** b: 11/3/1921; m: 11/23/1941 - House wife
									11	**David Pitre, Sr** b: 10/30/1942; d:1/7/2005 Delcambre - Carpenter specializing in Shrimp Boats
									11	**Bryan Pitre, Sr** b: 08/02/1945; Carpenter/Mechanic specializing in Shrimp Boats
								10	**Doris Pitre** b: 4/12/1926; m: 12/7/1941; d: 12/2/1997 Houma
								10	**Lee Roy J.Pitre, Sr**. b: 4/12/1928; d: 10/14/2006 Lafayette LA - Master Carpenter specializing in cabinets
								III	1st wife **Betty Jean (Fabacher)** b: 11/6/1933; d: 10/29/2000 [Leo P Fabacher]
									11	**Debra (Pitre) Carroll** b: 8/8/1951 Lafayette, professional educator
									2nd wife **Anna Lou (Theriot)** b: 8/24/1928; m: 2/3/1960; [Luke Theriot, Sr/Louise Cormier] Housewife
									11	**Lee Roy J. Pitre, Jr.** b: 7/14/1960 Lafayette, Information Technology Consultant
									11	**Jarvis J. Pitre** b: 10/31/1964 Lafayette - Owner Pitre's Playsets - carpenter
									11	**Eric D. Pitre** b: 12/23/1965 Lafayette; Computer consultant/Analyst

Jean Pitre b: Abt. 1636 "d'origine flamande"; d: Abt. 1689 Port Royal, Acadia
+Marie Pesseley b: Abt. 1645 Port Royal; m: Abt. 1665 Port Royal ; d: 12/26/1707 Port Royal
    [Isaac/Barbe Bajolet]

(2-I)   **Marie Pitre** b: Abt. 1666 Port Royal; d: Aft. 1726
        +Francois Amireau dit Tourangeau b: Abt. 1644; m: Abt. 1683 Port Royal; d: Aft. 1726

(2-II)   **Catherine Pitre** b: Abt. 1668 Port Royal; d: Bet. 1706 - 1714 Acadia
        +Claude Bertrand b: Abt. 1651; m: Abt. 1685 Port Royal; d: Abt. 1726 Acadia

(2-III)   **Claude Jean Pitre** b: Abt.02/1671 Port Royal, Acadia; d: 1752 Port Royal, Acadia
        +Marie Anne Comeau b: Abt.1678 Acadia; m: Abt.1696 Port Royal; d: 07/09/1707 Port Royal
            [Pierre/Jeanne Bourg];
                Children: Francine & Angelique (twins) b. 1707
        +Anne Jeanne Henry {2[ND] wife} b:Abt.1688 Mines; m:02/17/1710 Port Royal; d:11/29/1757 Quebec
            [Robert/Marie Madeleine Godin];

(2-IV)   **Marc Pitre** b: Abt.1673 Port Royal; d: Aft.1714
        +Jeanne Brun b: Abt.1676 Port RoyalAcadia; m: Abt. 1699 Acadia; d: Aft.1714
            [Sebastien/Huguette Bourg]

(2-V)   **infant Pitre** b: Abt. 1675 Port Royal; d: Aft. 1678 Port Royal

(2-VI)   **Pierre Pitre** b: Abt. 1677 Port Royal; d: Aft. 1700

(2-VII)   Jean Denis Pitre II b: Abt. 1680 Port Royal; d: 1799 Cobequid, Nova Scotia
        +Francoise Babin b: Abt. 1681 Port Royal; m: Abt. 1698 Port Royal; d: Aft. 1724
            [Antoine/Marie Mercier]

(2-VIII)   **Francois Pitre** b: Abt. 1682 Port Royal; d: 12/05/1725 Port Royal
        +Anne Prejean b: Abt. 1687 Port Royal; m: 07/27/1705 Port Royal
            [Jean/Andree Savoie]

(2-IX)   **Marguerite Pitre** b: Abt. 1683 Port Royal; d: 07/12/1747 Port Royal
        +Abraham Comeau b: Abt. 1680 Port Royal; m: Abt. 1701 Port Royal; d: Aft. 1739
            [Pierre/Jeanne Bourg]

(2-X)   **Jeanne Pitre** b: Abt. December 1685 Port Royal
        +Jean Pierre Piat dit La Bonte b: Abt. 1671; m: Abt. 1701 Acadia

(2-XI)   **Jeanne Pitre** b: Abt. 1688 Port Royal; d: Aft. 1707

---

[44] B – Born, M – Married, D – Died, Bef – Before, Aft – After, Bet - Between

Jean Denis Pitre b: Abt. 1680 Port Royal, Acadia; d: 1779
+Francoise Babin b: Abt. 1681 Port Royal, Acadia; m: Abt. 1698 Port Royal, Acadia; d: 1780 Cobequid
[Antoine Vincent Babin b.1625 d.1686 / Marie Joseph Mercier b.1645 d.1686]
The great majority of Pitre's who emigrated to Louisiana were descendants of Jean Denis Pitre.

(3-I) **Jean Baptiste Pitre** b: Abt. 1699 Cobequid, Acadia; d: 1758 at sea during the crossing to France
+Marguerite Theriot b:Abt.1701 Grand Pre, Acadia; m:Abt.721 Acadia; d:1758 at sea crossing
[Pierre/Marie Bourg];

(3-II) **Joseph Pitre** b:Abt.1700 Cobequit; d: Abt. 12/13/1758 shipwreck *Duke Williams* crossing to France
+Elisabeth (Isabelle) Boudrot b:Abt.1701 Acadia; m:Abt.1724 Acadia; d:12/13/1758 at sea
Children Michel, Madeline {husb. Louis Mathieu Doiron bap. Boston by Madeline's grandfather}, Cecile;
all died at sea;   [Rene/unknown]

(3-III) Claude Jean Pitre b: Abt. 1701 Acadia; d:Bef. 27 November 1759
+Marguerite Doiron b:Abt.1708 Acadia; m:Abt.1724 Cobequit; d: Bef.11/ 27/1759
[Noel/Marie Henry]

(3-IV) **Michel Pitre** b:Abt.1704 Cobequit; d:Abt.12/13/1758 at sea in the shipwreck of *Duke Williams*
+Marie Madeleine Doiron b:09/28/1707 Grand Pre; m:Abt.1727 Acadia; d:12/13/1758 at sea
[Noel/Marie Henry]

(3-V) **Madeleine Pitre** b:Abt.1706 Cap de Sable; d:Abt.12/13/1758 at sea shipwreck of *Duke Williams*
+Louis Mathieu Doiron b:02/01/1706 Boston, MA; m: Abt. 1726 Acadia; d: 12/13/1758 at sea
[Noel/Marie Henry]

(3-VI) **Anne Marie Pitre** b: Abt. 1707 Cobequit, Acadia
+Charles Lapierre b: Abt.1698 Les Mines, Acadia; m:Abt.1725 Acadia ; d: Bef: 1727
[Francois/Jeanne Rimbault]
+Mathieu Brasseur dit Lebrasseur {2nd Husband} b: Abt.1705 Grand Pre; m:Abt.1727 Cobequit
[Mathieu/Jeanne Celestin dit Bellemere]

(3-VII) **Cecile Pitre** b: Abt.1708 Cobequit; d: 12/13/1758 at sea shipwreck of *Violet* on way to France
+Joseph Lejeune b:07/20/1704 Port Royal; m: Abt.1727 Acadia; d: 12/13/1758 shipwreck of *Violet*
[Pierre/Marie Thibodeau];

(3-VIII) **Francoise Pitre** b: Abt. 1710 Cobequit, Acadia
+Joseph Boutin b: 04/30/1710 Grand Pre; m: Abt. 1731 Cobequit; d: 06/13/1755
[Joseph/Marie Marguerite Lejeune]

(3-IX) **Christine dite Catherine Pitre** b: Abt. 1712 Acadia; d: Bet. 1752 - 1761
+Joseph Henry dit le Petit Homme b: Abt.1707 Mines; m:Abt.1729 Acadia; d: Bef.01/27/1761
[Robert/Marie Madeleine Godin]

(3-X) **Germain Jean Pitre** b: Abt. 1714 Pisiquit; d:10/20/1764 Le Mirebalais, St. Domingue, West Indies
+Marie Josephe Girouard b:10/ 27/1717 Grand Pre; m:Abt.1736 Acadia; d:1/16/1764 West Indies
[Pierre/Marie Doiron]

(3-XI) **Charles Pitre** b: Abt. 1720 Acadia; d:1757 Île Saint Jean
+Anne Thibodeau b: Abt.1721 Pisiguit, Acadia; m:Abt.1745 Acadia d: Bet. 1763 - 1785 France
[Philippe/Isabelle (Elisabeth) Vincent]

(3-XII) **Amand Pitre** b: Abt. 1724 Acadia; d: 1787 Louisiana
+Genevieve Arsement b:Abt.1724 Pobomcoup, Cap Sable; m:Abt.1746 Cobequid; d:Abt.1784 France
[Pierre Claude/Marie Josephe Theriot]

Continuation of Jean Denis Pitre and Francoise (Babin) Family tree (3rd child)

Claude Jean Pitre b: Abt. 1701 Pubnico Nova Scotia; d: 11/27/1759 Mur, Cotes d'Armor, Bretagne, France
  +Marguerite Doiron b: Abt. 1708 Acadia; m: Abt. 1724 Cobequit; d: Bef.11/27/1759
      [Noel/Marie Henry]

(4-I)   Benjamin Pitre b: Abt.1725 Cobequit; d:09/30/1782 St. Pierre de Reze, Bretagne, France
         +Jeanne Moyse b:07/29/1714 Port Royal; m: Abt.1747 Acadia; d:1758 at sea crossing to France
             [Francois/Marie Brun]

(4-II)   **Claude Pitre** b: Abt. 1727 Cobequit; d: 02/26/1769 Mordreux, France
         +**Rosalie Landry** b: Abt. 1734 Acadia; m: 11/06/1752 Port Lajoie, Île Saint Jean; d: Bef. 1764
             [Joseph/Elizabeth Vincent]
         +**Marie Blanche Richard** {2^{ND} wife) b:Abt.1737 Acadia;m:09/25/1764 France; d:Aft.1791 Lafourche, LA
             [Pierre/Marie Boudrot]

(4-III) **Jean Baptiste Pitre** b: Abt. 1729 Beaubassin

(4-IV)   **Paul Hypolite Pitre** b: Abt. 1732 Cobequit, Acadia; d: 01/31/1767 St. Suliac, Bretagne, France
         +**Marguerite Louise Valet** b:12/15/1743 Île Saint Jean; m:2/8/1763 St. Suliac, France; d:Aft.1780
             [Louis Vallet dit Langevin/Marie Brigitte Pinet]

(4-V)   **Francois Pitre** b: Abt. 1734 Cobequit, Acadia; d:09/18/1762 Pleurtuit, France
         +**Ursule Breau** b: Abt.1740 Cobequit; m:03/18/1762 Pleurtuit, France; d:Bet.1791/1795 Lafourche
             [Joseph/Ursule Bourg]

(4-VI)   **Raphael Pitre** b: Abt. 1739 Cobequit, Acadia; d:06/30/1763 Mordreux, France

(4-VII) **Olivier Pitre** b: Abt. 1741 Cobequit, Acadia; d: Abt. 1784 France
         +**Marie Latreille Moyse** b:Abt.1738 Isle Royale; m:04/23/1763 Louisbourg; d:Bet.1810/1820 Lafourche
             [Louis/Marie Louise Petitpas]
             Children: Constant b.1776

(4-VIII) **Ambroise Pitre** b: Abt. 1746 Acadia; d:12/14/1758 Cherbourg, France

Benjamin Pitre b: Abt.1725 Cobequit, Acadia; d:09/30/1782 St. Pierre de Reze, Bretagne, France
+**Jeanne Moyse** b: 07/29/1714 Port Royal; m: Abt. 1747 Cobequid d:1758 at sea crossing to France
    [Francois Moyse / Marie Brun]

(5-I)   **Agnes Pitre** b: Abt. 1748 Cobequit, Acadia; d: Aft. 1798 Louisiana
       +**Joseph Guerin** b:Abt.1753 Acadia;m:04/30/1776 St.Similien,France;d:12/12/1813 Plattenville, LA
         [Dominique/Anne Leblanc]

(5-II)   **Francoise Pitre** b: Abt. 1749 Acadia; d: 1758 at sea during crossing to France

(5-III)   **Canute Pitre** b: Abt. 1755; d:1758 at sea during crossing to France

+Marguerite Marie Boudrot {2nd Wife} b:1741 Grand Pre Acadia; m:11/27/1759 La Gouesniere,Ille-et-Villaine, France;
    d:1806 Louisiana
    [Jean Baptiste Boudrot {Boudreaux} b.1718 d.1746 / Catherine Brassaud {Brasseaux} b.1719 d.1746]

(5-IV)   **Marie Pitre** b:11/25/1761 St. Suliac, Bretagne, France; d:12/02/1825 Thibodaux, LA
       +**Antoine Marin** b: Abt. 1746; m: Abt. 1787 Lafourche, LA; d: Bef. 1825

(5-V)   **Madeleine Modeste Pitre** b:07/ 22/1763 St. Suliac, Bretagne, France; d:10/26/1793 Plattenville, LA
       +**Jean Alain Gautrot** b:9/27/1764 Pleslin, Cotes du Nord, France; m:1/21/1786 St. Louis Cathedral, New Orleans
         [Alexandre/Marguerite Hebert]
       +**Antoine Renaud** {2nd Husband} b:Abt.1760 Bordeaux; m:08/17/1792 Donaldsonville LA; d:Aft.1793
         [Francois/Marie Berrinel]

(5-VI)   **Jean Baptiste Pitre** b:12/22/1765 St. Suliac, Bretagne, France; d:01/13/1767 St. Suliac, France

(5-VIII) **Cecile Olive Pitre** b:01/19/1768 St. Suliac, Bretagne, France; d: Aft.1788 Louisiana

(5-IX)   **Marguerite Charlotte Pitre** b:01/25/1770 St. Suliac, Bretagne, France; d:10/03/1807 Lafourche, LA
       +**Armand Philipe Fremin** b:Abt.1768 Chantenay, Bretagne, France; m:2/14/1787 Donaldsonville, LA
         d: Bet. September 1808-1820
         [Armand/Anne Taunee]
         Children: Lorenzo b.1780, Juan Bautista b.1786, Laurent b.1788, Jean Baptiste b.1794

(5-X)   **Francois Jean Baptiste Pitre** b:8/12/1773 St. Suliac, France; d:9/20/1781 St. Pierre de Reze, France

(5-XI)   **Genevieve Louise Pitre** b:07/17/1775 Vienne, France; d:09/09/1777 St. Pierre de Reze, France

(5-XII) **Etienne Pitre** b: Abt. 06/04/1778 France; d: Bet. 1785 - 1788 Louisiana, never married

(5-XIII) Jean Pitre b: Abt. 10/02/1780 [Nantes] St. Pierre de Reze, Bretagne, France; d:Bet.1813-1832 Ascension,
LA
       +Marie Reine Bourg b: Abt.11/17/1789 Donaldsonville, LA; m:09/01/1808 Donaldsonville;
         d:11/10/1832 Thibodaux, LA
         [Jean/Catherine Viaud]

(5-XIV) **Mathurin Pitre** b: Abt.01/24/1783 Nantes, France; d:02/03/1783 Nantes, France

Continuation of Benjamin Pitre and Marguerite (Boudrot) 2nd wife Family tree (12th child)

Jean Baptiste Pitre b: Abt.10/02/1780 St. Pierre de Reze, Bretagne, France; d:Abt. 1817 Ascension, LA
+Marie Reine Bourg b: Abt. 11/17/1789 Donaldsonville, LA; m:09/01/1808 Donaldsonville, settled on upper bayou;
　　　d:11/10/1832 St Joseph Church, Thibodaux, LA
　　　　　[Jean Cecile Bourg b.1760 France / Catherine Viaud b.1748]

(6-I)　Jean Florentin Pitre b:03/31/1811 Plattenville, Assumption Parish, LA; d:10/27/1886 Thibodaux, LA
　　　+Marie Modeste Azelie Thibodeaux b: 1/31/1812 Plattenville, LA; m:7/23/1832 Thibodaux;
　　　　　d: Abt. 1839 Thibodaux, LA
　　　　　[Jean Baptiste Thibodeaux/Martine Hache]
　　　+Susanne Zulmie Toups {2nd Wife} b:10/8/1816 Plattenville m:8/31/1840 St. Joseph, Thibodaux;
　　　　　d: Aft.1880
　　　　　[Drauzin Joseph/Judith Mayer]

(6-II)　**Rosalie Leanor Pitre** b: 08/06/1813 Plattenville, LA; d: 11/10/1888 Thibodaux, LA
　　　+Nicolas Arcement b:3/3/1802 Plattenville, LA; m:5/26/1834 St. Joseph, Thibodaux
　　　　　d:01/29/1862 Thibodaux, LA
　　　　　[Tranquille Francois/Anne Margueritte Rassicot]

Jean Florentin Pitre b:03/31/1811 Plattenville, LA; d: (76) 10/27/1886 Thibodaux, LA, Field Laborer
Funeral on 10/27/1886 at St Joseph church in Thibodaux by Reverend C. Favre
+Marie Modeste Azélie **Thibodeau** b:1/31/1812 Plattenville; m:7/23/1832 Thibodaux; d:Abt.1839 Thibodaux
[Jean Baptiste Thibodeau / Martine Hache]

(7-I)   **Florentin Marcel Pitre** b:01/16/1834 Thibodaux, LA; d: 09/04/1845 Thibodaux, LA

(7-II)   **Jean Aurélien Pitre** b: 02/11/1837 Thibodaux, LA; d: 7/26/1848 Thibodaux, LA

(7-III)   **Marcellite Elise Pitre** b: 10/14/1838 Thibodaux, LA; d: Aft.1850 Barataria, Jefferson, LA

+Susanne Zulmie Toups {2nd Wife} b:10/08/1816 Plattenville; m:08/31/1840 St. Joseph, Thibodaux;d.Aft.1880
{64yo}

[{German Creole} Drauzin Joseph Toups b.1783 des allemands LA d.12/07/1835 /
(Judique Maillard? b.1785 Des Allemands, LA; m.02/15/1808 st John, Edgar, LA;
d.05/30/1847 Thibodaux LA) Judith Mayer]

(7-IV)   Élie Pierre Pitre b: 08/26/1841 Thibodaux; d: 04/19/1898 Montegut
+ - Jambon {1st wife}
+ Cornelia Mathilda White {2nd wife} b:10/7/1850 Houma, LA; m:9/13/1873 Montegut; d:04/29/1934 Montegut
[Daniel William / Eliza Pierce]

(7-V)   **Joseph Aiser {Aupere} Pitre** b: 03/28/1843 Thibodaux; d: Aft. 1880
+Marie Celanie Adam b: 10/1/1847 Caminadaville, LA; m:5/14/1866 Our Lady of Peace, Vacharie,LA
d: Aft. 1900
[Jacques / Celanie Navare]
+{2nd wife} Marie Célanie m. 05/1866 Vacherie Church, St. James Parish[French Creole Jacques Adam]

(7-VI)   **Louis Jean Olésime Pitre** b: 04/05/1845 Thibodaux; d: Aft. 1850 Barataria, Jefferson, LA

(7-VII)   **Pierre William Pitre** b: 06/02/1848 Thibodaux, LA; d: 10/21/1867 Thibodaux, LA, never married

(7-VIII)   **Charles Lucien Pitre** b: 07/03/1853 Raceland, LA; d: 04/15/1934 Kraemer, LA
+Marie Estelle Adam b:10/19/1853 Raceland; m:02/15/1876 St. Joseph, Thibodaux;
d:Bet.1880-1883 Lafourche
[Jean Marie / Zeolide Rodrigue]

+Julia Ford {2nd Wife} b: 07/1864 Lafourche; m: 06/27/1883 St. Joseph, Thibodaux;
d:03/31/943 Lafourche
[Joseph / Louise Thibodeau]

(7-IX)   **Marie Pitre** b: 04/12/1859 Lafourche, LA; d: Bef. 1920
+Julien Henri Larousse b: 09/03/1867 Lafourche; m: 01/31/1889 Lockport, LA;
d:09/23/1931 Thibodaux, LA
[Victor Hippolite / Felicite Marie Martin]

(7-X)   **Drauzin Pitre** b: 11/1860 Lafourche, LA; d: Aft. 1900
+Eliska Lepine b:01/1869 Lafourche; m:5/4/1889 Lockport, LA; d: Aft. 1900
[Charles / Amy]

Continuation of Jean Florentin Pitre and Susanne Zulmie (Toups) Family tree (4th child)

Elie Pierre Pitre b: 11/26/1841 Thibodaux, LA; d: (56) 04/19/1898
        complications inflammatory rheumatism Bayou Terrebonne
        Funeral at Sacred Heart, Montegut on April 20, 1898; Buried at Sacred Heart Cemetery in Montegut
+ Jambon {1st wife}
+ Cornelia Mathilda White {2nd wife} b:10/07/1853; bap.09/25/1854 Houma; m:09/13/1873 Montegut; d:04/29/1934; Dugas Cemetery

        [Cornelia Parents; Daniel William White b.10/111804 Aurelius, Cayuga County, NY; d.aft.1873, carpenter];
        Eliza Pierce b.1815 Iberville; m.aft 1846; d.04/28/1900 Montegut. Eliza was short for Elizabeth;
        Madeleine's parents were Jacque Cantrelle and Melanie Picou;
        Eliza Pierce parents: Daniel L Pierce b.1787 Westmoreland Pennsylvania; d.11/13/1827 New Orleans;
        Mary Elizabeth Sons [Sans] b.1795 New Hampshire; d.02/18/1819 Thibodaux LA]

(8-I)   **Jemmy Joseph Pitre** b:06/17/1874 Montegut; d: 11/20/1886 Montegut; Died of blood poisoning after spider bite

(8-II)   John Lee Pitre b:06/02/1876 bap.09/29/1876 Montegut; d:08/041965 Chauvin
      + Francis Marie Autin b: 3/29/1879 Montegut; m: 05/05/1896 Houma; d:12/04/1953 Chauvin
      [Charles Autin {Spanish b.1840 Thib. / Lucie Marie Vitto {Italian} b.11/29/1843 Thib.; d.10/29/1885 Houma]

(8-III) **Lenius Élie "Lee" Pitre** b:05/01/1878 Montegut; d:03/15/1970 Montegut; 1920 farm laborer; 1930 river pilot
      +Marie Lea Julienne Rhodes b:11/24/1877 Montegut; m:04/27/1899 Montegut;
          d:04/27/1932 Montegut
          [Simon Robert / Marie Zulmie Robichaux]
          Children: Camile, Andrew, Allen, Millar, Rosemary, Bruce, Leola (Pitre){b.1916}/Clarence David, Morris

(8-IV) **Richard Peter Pitre** b:02/ 21/1880 Montegut; d: Bet. 1920-1930 Montegut
      +Julienne Leboeuf b: Abt. 1882 Montegut; m: Abt. 1902 Montegut; d: 12/14/1950 Montegut
          [Etienne] Children: Clarence J. b.1916 d.12/21/1989

(8-V)   **Joseph Daniel Forest Pitre** b: 01/03/1883 {baptized 08/20/1883} Montegut; d: 04/01/1967 Montegut;
          6ft tall; 1920 Oil field driller; 1930 trapper/fur-trader;   Latter Tomb headstone maker
      +Bertha Mary Breaux b:02/20/1895 Montegut; m:01/18/1913 Terrebonne; d:03/19/1967 Montegut
          [Horace Rogers / Lucie Chauvin]
          Children: Horace; James; Norris; Lionel Patrick b.03/17/1929, 6ft tall; Rosalie (Pitre) Crochet; Lucy Mahan

(8-VI) **Elesse 'Ellis' Random Pitre** b. 03/08/1885 Montegut; d: 09/18/1978 Houma;
          lived in mud house with no floor lower Terrebonne bayou;
          1920 oil field laborer; 1930 janitor/oil production dept;
      +Marie Ernestine Cunningham b: 04/08/1885 Montegut; m:2/9/1916 Montegut; d:03/30/1951 Houma
          Lived in mud house near Texaco south of Montegut
          [Robert Clement / Marie Hebert];
          Children: Mable Marie b.06/03/1918 d.05/13/2007, Bessie Marie b.12/25/1919 d.06/08/1969, Roscia, Viola
Josephine b.03/05/1923 d.03/18/2005

(8-VII) **Cordelia Camilia Pitre** b: 11/1888 Montegut; d: 07/06/1988 Houma
      +Ludgar Jean Rhodes b: 8/15/1885 Montegut; m:1/30/1909 St. Francis de Sales, Houma;
          d:05/1975 Houma; [William / Elmire Josephine Guidry] Child. Beatrice 1910; Thelma 1912; Percy 1914

(8-VIII) **Amanda Josephine 'Mandy' Pitre** b: 09/18/1892 Montegut; d: 01/1978 Houma;
      + **Sidney George Champagne** b: 12/22/1887 Thibodaux, LA; m:01/19/1911 St Ann Church, Bourg;
          d:12/30/1936 Houma
          [Charles Joseph / Eve Cecile Guidry]
          Child: Aurely 1913; Ethel 1916; Roland 1918; Vernon 1921; Gilford 1923; Sidney 1925; Betty 1929; Raymond 1930

(8-IX) **Mary Amy "Annie" Pitre** b: 04/04/1895 Montegut; d: 01/08/1930 Montegut
      +Claude Naquin b: Abt. 1895 Montegut; m: 01/04/1916 Houma; d: 06/13/1960 Montegut
          [Naquin / Josephine]
          Children: Elena 1918; Ruby 1919

Continuation of Élie Pierre Pitre and Mathilda Cornelia (White) Family tree (2nd child)

John Lee Pitre b: 06/02/1876 bap.09/29/1876 Montegut; d: 08/04/1965 in New Orleans; 5' 2" tall
 Congestive Heart Failure due to Arteriosclerotic heart disease, buried St Joseph Cemetery in Chauvin
+Francis Marie Autin b: 03/29/1879 Montegut; m: 5/5/1896{06/30/1949} Houma; d: 12/04/1953 in Chauvin; 4' 10" tall
 buried St Joseph Cemetery Chauvin
 [Charles Henry Autin b.1840 (river boat pilot) / Eliza Louise "Lucie" Marie {Viteaux} Vitto {Italian} b.1843 d.1885]
 [Lucie's parents; Fortunate Vito & Cleonies Waguespak]

(9-I)   **Wisteria Marie Pitre** b:01/03/1897 Montegut; d: 06/26/1984 Chauvin; 4' 10" tall, 6th Grade
 +James "Jim" Eugene Carlos b:07/28/1889 Spain; m: 08/21/1915 Montegut; d: Bef. 06/1984
  [James/Marie Carrere] Rosalie Carlos & Irvin LeBoeuf : Children : Mary , Jude, Barry, Larry,
   Janet Carlos & Angelo Roberts Babin

(9-II)   Élie Joseph Pitre b:02/08/1898 Montegut; 4th Grade, d:06/24/1978 Delcambre; St Joseph Cemetery Chauvin
 +Leona Addie LeBoeuf b:1/30/1900 Montegut; m:01/21/1921 Houma; d:08/15/1934 Chauvin;
  St Joseph Cemetery; [Beattie Paul Lebouefb.1873 / Olympia Aimee Hebert b.1874]

(9-III) **Howard Joseph Pitre** b: 11/29/1899 Montegut; d: Abt.1928 Chauvin
 +Valerie Babin b: 5/23/1906 Chauvin; m:01/02/1922 Houma; d:12/13/1962 Chauvin
  [John Francis/Eva Guidry] Kids: Medaline Pitre Married Buffin LeBlanc; Harry Pitre m.Mavis Charponter

(9-IV)   **America Marie Pitre** b:05/18/1902 Montegut; d:01/27/1987 Chauvin
 +Ruffin Charles Lecompte b: 6/10/1897 Chauvin; m:01/11/1919 Sacred Heart, Montegut, LA;
  d:12/05/1975 Chauvin
  [Nicholas/Elodie Chauvin] Kids:Dority, Percy, Aubrey, Lester, Chester, Barbra, Charles, Cyrus, Helen b.1924

(9-V)   **Emelie "Emily" Marie Pitre** {2nd wife of CD Long} b:01/23/1904 Montegut; d:09/12/1993 St Joseph Cem; 5th Grade
 +Charles Dennis Long b: Abt.1904; m: Abt. 1922; d:1928 pneumonia in new Orleans, 2nd Grade
  Kids: Emeline Harris (Long) Cunningham 6th Grade, Harry 4th Grade, Charles 2nd Grade, Dorthy

(9-VI)   **Anaise Marie Pitre** b:01/26/1906 Montegut; d:04/09/1993 Houma
 +Charles A. Savoie b: 07/13/1890 Lockport; m: 04/06/1923 Houma; d:08/14/1970 Houma
  [Beauregard Louis/Aglae Marie Roger] Kids: Elain Savoie married Wilmer Babin – Lind Babin, Laurie Babin

(9-VII) **Rosena Anna Pitre** b:04/29/1908 Chauvin; d:07/07/1998 Montegut
 +William Stanley Robichaux b:07/21/1902 Montegut; m: 02/20/1930 Montegut; d:02/09/1988 Montegut
  [Paul Augustin/Azema Elizabeth Robichaux] Kids: Druby Robicheaux, Wilbert Robicheaux, Robert Robicheaux

(9-VIII) **Lorena Pitre** b: Abt. 1895 or 1910 Chauvin; d: Bef. 1920; 17 months old when died

(9-IX)   **Eldora M. Pitre** b:07/01/1912 Chauvin; d:04/26/2004 San Antonio, Bexar, TX, 7th Grade
 +Davidson Keefe b:Abt.1895; m:Aft.1940; d: Bef. 04/2004; Kids: Mary Kieef married Micheal Brown

(9-X)   **Frances Theresa Pitre** b:10/27/1914 Chauvin; d:09/15/2001 Bourg, LA
 +Norris G. Leboeuf b:03/15/1912 Bourg; m:Abt.1935 Chauvin; d:04/30/2004 Bourg
  [Oleus / Julie Hebert] Kids: Roberta (LeBouef) married James Duplantis {Brad, Francien, Kelly}

(9-XI)   **John Henry Pitre Jr** b:1917 Chauvin, Terrebonne, LA; d: 3/9/1961; 1940 carpenter/boat builder
  Diseal mechanic; Died at kitchen table
 +Aline Prosperie b:12/13/1918 Montegut; m: Abt.1938; d: 8 May 2001 Chauvin
  [Michel / Maggie Lecompte] Kids: Soris Pitre, Cyrus Pitre, Carylin Pitre, Lucy Mae Pitre

(9-XII) **Cornelia Pitre** b:01/06/1920 Chauvin; d:05/18/2010 Houma
 +Ernest Portier b:08/08/1916 Chauvin; m: Abt. 1939; d: 05/1985 Chavin; Kids: Gladis Portier, Renard Portier

(9-XIII) **Marguerite Penny Pitre** b:10/27/1923 Chauvin d:06/26/2009 Laplace, St. John the Baptist, LA, 7th Grade
 +Albert Pitre {1st Husband}   +Yank Rome {2nd Husband} ; Kids: Albert Pitre Jr, Ysconne Pitre

Élie Joseph Pitre b: 02/08/1898 bap. 04/29/1899 Sacred Heart Church Montegut; d:06/24/1978 in Erath Hospital ;
      5' 0" tall, blue eyes, light brown hair, 4th Grade
      cerebrovascular accident due to coronary disease,
      buried in St Joseph cemetery in Chauvin Louisiana
+Leona Addie (Eddie) LeBoeuf b:01/30/1900 Montegut; m:02/02/1921 Sacred Heart Church by Reverend Jos. Pierre;
      d: 08/20/1934 lung cancer in Chauvin;
      buried St Joseph Cemetery Chauvin
      [Beattie Paul / Olympia Aimee Hebert]

      +Maggie Richard b: 1881 ; d:4/12/1940 (who is this? Wrong person. Location of Leona's small granite headstone)
      +Aggie Marie Dupre {2[nd] wife} b:1/13/1911; m:12/12/1937 Sacred Heart; d:08/21/1951
      +Lawerence Goutierrez {3[rd] wife} m.11/21/1953; d. 1950
      +Nettie Gray Martin {4[th] wife} m. 01/19/1960 Delcambre; d. unknown

(10-I)   **Wilbert James Pitre** b:03/07/1923 Chauvin; d:03/30/2006 Delcambre, LA, 7th Grade
      +Hilda Boudelouche b:11/03/1921; m: 11/23/1941; d:03/02/2007 Delcambre
          [Clifford Boudloche / Emma Mazarac]
          David John Pitre b. 10/30/1942 Houma Married Ruth Cheamie m.11/30/1963; David Jr, Zachary, Patrick
          Bryan Joseph Pitre b. 08/02/1945 Houma; m08/02/1969 Sandra LeBlanc; Bryan Jr, Stacie

(10-II)   **Doris M. Pitre** b:12/07/1925 Houma; d:07/23/1997 Houma;
      + VJ Malbrough
          Patrick b. 8/271947
          Peter b. 10/01/1957
          Percy b.12/27/1952
          Polly b.08/16/1954
          Paula b.08/20/1956
          Pivs b.12/08/1958
          Paul b.10/28/1961

(10-III)   Lee Roy James Pitre Sr b: 04/12/1928 Houma; d:10/14/2006 Lafayette, LA;
      brown hair, steel blue eyes, 5' 4" tall, 7th Grade
      +Betty Jane Fabacher {1[st] wife} b.11/06/1933; m.12/24/1949; div.1955; red hair
          Kids: Debra (Pitre) Carroll
      +Anna Lou Theriot {2[nd] wife} b:08/24/1928; m:06/03/1960
          {Anna Lou 1st marriage 1945; div.1959}
          [Luke Theriot / Louise Cormier]
              Kids: Lee Roy Pitre, Jr, Jarvis Pitre, Eric Pitre

Notes for Élie Joseph Pitre:
Census
- 1930 Terrebonne, Louisiana: Élie J. Pete 32, wife Leona A. 30, Wilbert J. 7, Doris M. 4 years 3 months, Leeroy J. 1 year 11 months.

- 1940 Terrebonne, LA: Élie Pitre 42 contractor boat builder/self boat builder, wife Aggie 29, Wilbert 17 deckhand/Voohies tug boat, Doris 14, LeRoy 12. [Little Caillou Route]

WWI registration records: Élie Joseph Pitre; Terrebonne, LA; born 8 Feb 1898; Mother: Francis Autin Pitre; short height, medium build; blue eyes & light brown hair.

Daniel White Nettleton[45] b.10/11/1803 Aurelius, New York, d.bet.1860 & 1868;   Carpenter
    [Parents: Enos G. Nettleton b. Cayouga county, New York / Grace Maria Smith]
    Fought with the Company of Sabine Volunteers in Texas for freedome from Mexico.

Melanie Madeleine Cantrelle, 1st wife, b., m.02/18/1829 in Thibodaux; d.abt 1845

SOUTH LOUISIANA RECORDS, Vol 1, pages 138 and 414
Daniel Nettleton, about 25 years old, from Cayuga County, New York,
son of deceased Enos Nettleton and deceased Grace Maria Smith,
married 18 Feb 1829 to Melanie Cantrelle, about 18 years old, dau of Jacques Cantrelle and Melanie Picou.
[Thibodaux Courthouse Marriage Volume 1, #1].

        Daniel & Melanie's children
            Marie Melicere Nettleton, daughter, b.12/24/1831, Thibodaux
            Melanie Victorie Nettleton, daughter, b.04/18/1833 in Thibodaux
            Marie Madeleine Nettleton, daughter, b.12/24/1834 in Thibodaux
            Daniel William Nettleton Jr, son, b.11/07/1836 in Thibodaux
            Sarah Ann Nettleton, daughter, b.06/15/1842 in Thibodaux

Eliza (Pierce) Price, Daniel's Girlfriend, b. 02/28/1815 Iberville; Cohabitation 1846; d.04/28/1900 Montegut
        [Farther: Daniel Pierce; Mother: Mary Elizabeth Sons]
        Eliza's 1st Husband John Joseph Price b.1794 Fredric County, Virgina; m.03/16/1834 LaFourche parish

    Eliza & John Price's children
        William Franklin Price b.01/16/1835 in Thibodaux
        John Wallace Price b.09/01/1837in Thibodaux
        Josephine Price b.07/17/1839 in Thibodaux
        Oscar Horckar Danaiff Price b.09/15/1841 (Church; v. 1-a.p50)
        Amanda Melvina Price b.01/03/1846 in Thibodaux

    Eliza Price & Daniel White's children
        Charles, son, b.1847
        California Louisia , daughter, b.1849
        Osiah, son, b.1852
        Cornelia Mathilda, daughter, b.10/07/1853
        Malvina, daughter, b.1856

---

[45] Nettleton graves http://files.usgwarchives.net/la/terrebonne/cemeteries/dugas.txt

1899/10/20   Daniel W. Nettleton, US Civil war pension index

1840   Census
               Daniel Nettleton, LaFourche parish

1844 (06/13/1844)[46] Land conveyance record
               LaFourche Township 17-S, Range 21-E, Section 7, 49.8 acres
               Land purchased signed by "Daniel Nettleton"

1850   Census
               Daniel Nettleton, 48yo, Elisa 36, Sugar Census Index, Bayou LaFourche left bank
               Daniel & Melanie's children: Zavier16, Sarah 6, Charlesdon 5, California 3,
               Eliza & John Price's children: Uallan Price 14, Josephine Price 12, Hosckar Price 8, James Price 10

South LA Records vol. 3 p. 388
Nettleton, Daniel children listed: Sarah; Daniel. Bond of tutor: 26 May 1855 (Thib Ct Hse.: Succ. #211)

1860/07/11   Census
               Daniel White, 38yo, Carpenter, House $400, Ward 8, Terrebonne,
               Eliza 40, wife
               Children: Charles 13, Calofornia 11, Osiah 8, Cornnilia 6, Malvina 4
               North Central edge of Terrebonne parish, Right bank Bayou LaFourche, west present day Thibadaux
                Next Door to Henry b.1822 & Josephine 21yo White,
               2nd homestead from John & Henrietta Rhodes

1868/11/09   Steamer Trade Wind, Passenger list
               Port of Departure: Belize
               Port of Arrival: New Orleans ; Arrival 11/09/1868
               National Archives Series Number: M259_53

               Henry White, male, 38, mechanic
               Janie? White, female, 23
                Robert White, male, age 12
                Richard White, male age 10
                Emaline White, female, age 8
                Virginia, female, age 6
                E. Price, age 50, female (Eliza)
                C. Price, age 14, female (Cornelia)
                Sheldon, Price, age 18, male (Shelton Charles)
                O. Price, age 14, male (Ozias)
                M. Price, age 11, female (Malvina)
                Note: C. Price is probably Cornelia who is still single. Louise "California" is married prior to this trip. (CFD)

1870   Census   Charles Nettleton next door to Henry White

               Sheldon Charles Nettleton b.02/15/1847 b.01/10/1873, some schooling
               +Victorine Eveline Domingue

               Calafornia White b.1847, some schooling
               Osiah White b.1849, some schooling
               Cornelia White b.1853
               Malvina White b.1856

---

[46] Nettleton Land http://search.ancestry.com/cgi-bin/sse.dll?db=BLMlandpatents&h=770855&indiv=try&o_vc=Record:OtherRecord&tid=877643&tpid=1228015363&rhSource=3550

Steamer Trade Winds, Port of Belize Honduras

Henry White

Eliza Price (Daniel White's

Cornelia (Price) White

185

November 9, 1868

REFERENCES

An Acadian Parish remembered, The registers of Saint Jean-Baptiste, Annapolis Royal, 1702-1755. In *Nova Scotia Archives*. Retrieved from http://www.gov.ns.ca/nsarm/cap/acadian/ default.asp "Search Results: Pitre"; Microfilm retrieval code: mfm 22623

Bocage, C.W. (1915). Bocage's official map of the Parish of Terrebonne, Louisiana. Library of Congress Geography and Map Division. Washington, D.C. 20540-4650 USA. Retrieved from http://www.loc.gov/item/2013593065; http://memory.loc.gov/cgi-bin/query/h?ammem/ gmd:@field(NUMBER+@band(g4013t+ct001200))

Bradshaw, J. (2011, May 13). Great flood of 1927. Retrieved February 20, 2013 from *KnowLA Encyclopedia of Louisiana*: http://www.knowla.org/entry.php?rec=763

Brasseaux, C. A. (1991). *Scattered to the wind: Dispersal and wanderings of the Acadians, 1755-1809*. Lafayette, LA: The Center for Louisiana Studies, University of Southwestern Louisiana.

Bujold, N., & Caillebeau, M. (1979). *Les origines françaises des premières familles acadiennes*. Edited by the Conseil Général of Vienna, Austria.

Canadian National Archives (1905). *Sieur de la Roque 1752 Census for Prince Edward Island/Île Saint Jean*. Report of the Canadian Archives for 1905, pp 75-165.

Cormier, S. A. (2007). *Acadians who found refuge in Louisiana. February 1764 – early 1800's*. retrieved from http://www.acadiansingray.com/Appendices-ATLAL-PITRE.htm#PITRE

Cormier, S. A. (2007). *Ships of the Acadian expulsion, 1755 and 1758*. Retrieved from http://www.acadiansingray.com/Appendices-Ships,%201755-58.htm

Cornelia Mathilda White (2014). In *Authement, Fatchett, Savoie, Daigle Connection*. Retrieved from http://wc.rootsweb.ancestry.com/cgi-bin/igm.cgi?op=GET&db=cynthiadaigle&id=I015992#s1

Crochet (Pitre), R. (2013, October). Personal interview. Montegut, LA.

Cunningham (Long), E. (April 30, 2013). Personal interview. Chauvin, LA.

D'etiveaud, H. (1981). *Cajan heritage: Recipes, history, poems, voodoo, humor.* Owensboro, KY: McDowell Publications.

Davis (Pitre), L. (October 2013). Personal interview. Metairie, LA.

D'Entremont, C. J. (Spring, 1979). The Acadian census of 1678. Translation and interpretation. *French Canadian and Acadian Genealogical Review, 2* (1), pp. 47-66.

Dugas, J. B. (December 25, 2012). *The hermit of Montegut.* Retrieved from http://www.findagrave.com/cgi-bin/fg.cgi?page=gr&GRid=102634792

Duplantis (Pitre), R. (January 26, 2013). Personal interview. Bourg, LA.

Faragher, J. (2005). *A great and noble scheme.* New York, NY: W.W. Norton & Company.

Guidry, Sh. (1970). *Le Terrebonne. A History of Montegut.*

Johnston, O. M. (February, 1906). Sources of the lay of the two lovers. *Modern Language Notes, 21*(2), pp. 34-39. Baltimore, MD: The Johns Hopkins University Press. Retrieved from http://www.jstor.org/stable/2917732. doi: 10.2307/2917732

Kiesel, J.(2007). *Images of America – Lafayette.* Martinez, CA: Arcadia Publishing. Retrieved from http://www.cocohistory.org /book-lafayette.html

Kinoshita, Sh., & McCracken, P. (2012). Marie de France. A critical companion. Cambridge, MA: Boydell & Brewer.

Lebergott, S. (1960). Wage trends, 1800-1900.Trends in the American economy in the nineteenth century. Retrieved on January 17, 2012 from http://www.nber.org/chapters/c2486.pdf

Louisiana v. Mississippi – 202 U.S. 1 (1906). In Justia US Supreme Court. Retrieved from http://supreme.justia.com/cases/federal/us/202/1/case.html

Louisiana, Deaths Index, 1850-1875, 1894-1956.
Index, *FamilySearch* (https://familysearch.org/ pal:/MM9.1.1/FS1Z-5VL: accessed 03 Jun 2014), Elie Pitre in entry for Cornelia Pitre, 29 April 1934; citing Montegut, Terrebonne, Louisiana, certificate number 4803, State Archives, Baton Rouge; FHL microfilm 2113573.

Maps of Louisiana. (2014). Retrieved from http://www.mapofus.org/louisiana/

Melanson, A. (July, 2013). Personal interview. Annapolis Royal, Nova Scotia, Canada.

Melanson, W. (July 22, 2013). Personal Interview. Annapolis Royal, Nova Scotia, Canada.

Perez, L. X. Ship arrivals at St. Malo. Retrieved from http://froux.pagesperso-orange.fr/St_malo_arrivees/index_arrivee.htm

Pitre, B., Sr. (February 08, 2014). Personal interview. Delcambre, LA.

Pitre, É. (1970-1978). Personal communication. Delcambre, LA.

Pitre, F. J. (July 22, 2013). Clementsport, Nova Scotia, Canada.

Pitre, L. P. (October 2013). Personal interview. Montegut, LA.

Pitre, Lee Roy, Sr. (1970- 2006). Personal communication. Lafayette, LA.

Pitre, W. (1970 – 2006). Personal communication. Delcambre, LA.

Read, M. (1981, January 6). *Mrs. Carlos Relishes Life.* Interview, *The Courier.*

Retail prices of selected foods in U.S. cities, 1890-2011. (2005). Retrieved in February, 2013 from http://www.infoplease.com/ipa/A0873707.html

Rieder, M. P. & Rieder, N. G. (1967). *The Acadians in France, 1762-1776.* Metairie, LA.

Riley, F.L. (1904). *Publications of the Mississippi Historical Society. 8*, p. 327. Oxford, MS.

Robichaux, A. (1980). *Colonial settlers along Bayou LaFourche 1770-1798.* Louisiana: Hebert Publications. 1980

Rushton, W. (1979). The Cajuns from Acadia to Louisiana. New York, NY: Farrar Straus Giroux.
Sacred Heart Catholic Church. (2001). Montegut, LA.

Soudelier (LeCompt), H. (February 23, 2013). Personal interview. Houma, LA.

The deportation of the Acadians. (1986). Minister of Supply and Services, Canada.

U.S. Census Bureau (2011). *Historical statistics of the United States: Colonial times to 1970.* Bicentennial Edition, Part 2. Washington, D.C. Retrieved from http://fraser.stlouisfed.org/ docs/publications/histstatus/hstat1970_cen_1975_v2.pdf

United States General Index to Pension Files, 1861-1934. Index and images. *FamilySearch.* Retrieved in June, 2014 from http://FamilySearch.org. Citing NARA microfilm publication T288. Washington, D.C.: Veterans Administration, Publications Service, n.d.

Ville de Pîtres. (2013). Retrieved from http://www.villedepitres.fr/

Villere, S. L. (1972). *The Canary Islands migration to Louisiana, 1778-1783; the history and passenger lists of the Islenos volunteer recruits and their families.* Baltimore, MD: Genealogical Pub.

Helpful Research Websites and Resources

Acadian & Cajun genealogy & history. Retrieved from http://www.acadian-cajun.com

Acadian memorial. Retrieved from http://www.acadianmemorial.org/english/index.html

Acadian-Cajun genealogy & history. Retrieved from http://www.acadian-cajun.com/

Asrsenault, B. (1978). *Histoire et Genealogie de Acadiens.* Lemeac.

Commune. Retrieved from http://en.wikipedia.org/wiki/Communes_of_France

County of Flanders. Retrieved from http://en.wikipedia.org/wiki/County_of_Flanders

Cyr. Y. I. Acadian genealogy homepage. Retrieved from http://www.acadian.org/

Diocese of Baton Rouge, Catholic Church Records.

Family name. Retrieved from http://en.wikipedia.org/wiki/Family_name

Francois Roux. Retrieved from http://perso.wanadoo.fr/froux/divers/histoire.htm

History. Retrieved from http://www.blupete.com/History.htm
http://www.lexic.us/definition-of/toponymic.
http://www.merriam-webster.com/dictionary/toponymic;
http://www.thefreedictionary.com/toponymic;

King Charles the Bald. Retrieved from http://en.wikipedia.org/wiki/P%C3%AEtres

L'Ardoise genealogy. Retrieved from
http://lardoise.netfirms.com/index.html#L'Ardoise%20index

Louisiana and Cajun website directory. Retrieved from
http://www.louisianacajun.com/index.asp

Louisiana Department of Archives, Opelousas Colonial Documents, Baton Rouge, LA.

Marie de France (late 12th c.). Retrieved from
http://mockingbird.creighton.edu/english/fajardo/teaching/eng340/marie_de_fra
nce.htm

Marie de France. Retrieved from
http://archive.org/stream/mariedefrancesev00mari/mariedefrancesev00mari_djv
u.txt

Massignon Geneviève. *Les Parlers Français d'Acadie* is on file at the National
Archives of Paris.

Merovingian house Pîtres. Retrieved from http://www.angelfire.com/journal2/
ck15endtimecolumn/et9.html

Nova Scotia (2006). In *LoveToKnow Classic Encyclopedia.* Retrieved from
http://www.1911encyclopedia.org/Nova_Scotia

Nova Scotia, flag of (2007). In *Encyclopædia Britannica.* Retrieved from
http://www.britannica.com/eb/article-9105905>.

Ontario Genealogical Society. Retrieved from
http://www.ogs.on.ca/resources/first.html

PEI Baptismal Index. Government of Prince Edward Island. Retrieved from
http://www.edu.pe.ca/

Pitre family history. Retrieved from http://www.geocities.com/pitre_family.

Public Archives of Nova Scotia. Retrieved from
http://www.gov.ns.ca/nsarm/cap/acadian/ surnames.asp

Sieur de la Roque census of Île Saint Jean (now Prince Edward Island). (1752).
Retrieved from http://www.islandregister.com/1752.html/;
http://www.islandregister.com/pitre.html

Surnames derived from toponyms. Retrieved from http://en.wikipedia.org/wiki/
Category:Surnames_derived_from_toponyms

The Acadian Museum. Retrieved from http://www.acadianmuseum.com/

The Italian Historical Society of America. Retrieved from
http://www.italianhistorical.org/ verrazzano.htm. The section used with written
permission Giovanni Da Verrazzano.

The National Archives of Canada. Retrieved from http://www.archives.ca;
http://automatedgenealogy.com

The Provincial Archives of New Brunswick (PANB). Retrieved from
    http://archives.gnb.ca/Archives

Toponymic or occupational surnames. Retrieved from
    http://quizlet.com/2334250/patronymic-toponymic-or-occupational-surnames-
    flash-cards/

Toponymic. Retrieved from http://dictionary.reference.com/browse/toponymic;

Vien Ici. Retrieved from http://www.vienici.com

White, S. A. (1999). Dictionniare généalogique des familles acadiennes. Centre
    d'Etudes Acadiennes, Universite de Moncton.

Organizations providing Documentation and Authentication

Archdiocese of New Orleans, Archdiocesan Archives, 1100 Chartres Street, New Orleans, LA 70116-2596

Diocese of Baton Rouge Catholic Church Records (Diocese of Baton Rouge, Department of Archives, Baton Rouge, Louisiana)

Diocese of Houma-Thibodaux, Funeral and Cemetery records, 205 Audubon Avenue, Thibodaux, LA 70301

Genealogical Research Society of New Orleans, (*Genesis* Subscription only), P.O. Box 51791, New Orleans, La. 70151

Jefferson Parish Public Library, 2751 Manhattan Blvd., Harvey, LA 70058

La Societe des Cajuns, P.O. Box 581, Golden Meadow, LA 70357

Louisiana Genealogical and Historical Society, P.O. Box 3454, Baton Rouge, La. 70821

Louisiana State Archives and Records Section, P.O. Box 94125, Baton Rouge, LA 70804-9125

National Archives and Records Administration, General Reference Branch, 7th and Pennsylvania Avenue N.W., Washington, DC 20408

New Orleans Public Library, 219 Loyola Ave., New Orleans, LA 70140

Ontario Genealogical Society, 40 Orchard View Blvd. Suite 251, Toronto, Ontario M4R-1B9, Canada

Orlando Public Library, 101 E. Central Boulevard, Orlando, FL 32801-2407

Sacramental Records of the Roman Catholic Church of the Archdiocese of New Orleans (Archives of the Archdiocese of New Orleans, New Orleans, Louisiana)

Terrebonne Genealogy Society, P.O. 295, Station 2, Houma, LA 70380

Terrebonne Parish Library, 424 Roussel St., Houma, LA 70360

Additional Reading and Research Sources

Alexander, W. Jean & Secaire Jambon. Retrieved from http://trees.ancestry.com/tree/481595/person/-1960426002

Ancestors & Descendants of Élie Joseph Pitre. Retrieved from http://www.pitres.us/pitregenealogy ancestors.html

Chateauguay, Quebec (Ste. Barde) parish registers 1884-1899 (LDS film #1754022).

Chateauguay, Quebec (Ste. Martine) parish registers 1823-1836 (LDS film #1028329), 1836-1850 (LDS film #1028330), 1850-1860 (LDS film #1028331), 1860-1876 (LDS film #1028332) & 1877-1899 (LDS film #1754023).

Chateauguay, Quebec (Ste. Philomene, Mercier) parish registers 1840-1865 (LDS film #1031582), 1866-1876 (LDS film #1031583), 1877-1899 (LDS film #1753975).

Chénière Caminada, Jefferson, Louisiana. Retrieved from http://www.treasurenet.com/forums/louisiana/67968-grand-isle-cheniere-caminada.html

Chénière Caminada: The disappearance of a community. Retrieved from http://www.coast 2050.gov/reports/bia/ch2b.pdf

Digitized newspapers. Retrieved from http://guides.library.upenn.edu/historicalnewspapersonline

Fourth convoy. Retrieved from http://froux.pagesperso-orange.fr/divers/convoi4.htm#c11

Grand Isle. History. Retrieved from http://www.grandisle.us/

Great Mississippi Flood of 1927 (October 5, 2007). In *Wikipedia, the free encyclopedia*. Retrieved from http://en.wikipedia.org/w/index.php?title= Great_Mississippi_Flood_of_1927 &oldid=162541751

Hebert, D. J. *Acadian Families in Exile 1785*. Louisiana: Hebert Publications.

Hebert, D. J. *Acadians in Exile*. Louisiana: Hebert Publications.

Hebert, D. J. *Southwest Louisiana Records*. Louisiana: Hebert Publications.

Higgins Classic Boats Association. Retrieved from http://www.higginsclassicboats.org/ Web_Studio_Higgins_Website/History.html

Histoire de la marine Française. Retrieved from http://archive.org/details/histoiredelamari03larouoft

History of Belanger family. Founding of Belanger Canal (Bourg) & Madison Canal. Retrieved from http://kandrtell.tripod.com/gen/belanger.html

Hurricane Katrina. (January, 2008). In *Wikipedia, the free encyclopedia.* Retrieved from http://en.wikipedia.org/w/index.php?title=Hurricane_Katrina&oldid=181401586

Hurricane of 1909. Retrieved from http://en.wikipedia.org/wiki/1909_Atlantic_hurricane_season#Hurricane_Nine

Hurricane of August 6-16, 1860, Louisiana, Alabama, Mississippi. Retrieved from http://www.gendisasters. com/data1/la/hurricanes/hurricane-aug1860.htm

Hurricane Rita. (January, 2008). In *Wikipedia, the free encyclopedia.* Retrieved from http://en.wikipedia.org/w/index.php?title=Hurricane_Rita&oldid=180876029

Jim's Lost Pix. Retrieved from http://jamesfrey.com/alb_lost.htm

L'Amitié. Retrieved from http://froux.pagesperso-orange.fr/divers/amitiegf.jpg

Lafayette memories. Retrieved from https://www.facebook.com/groups/105642046143906/

Louisiane Acadien. Retrieved from https://www.facebook.com/groups/louisianeacadien/

Memories of Montegut, LA. Retrieved from https://www.facebook.com/groups/174422725963859/

Memories of Terrebonne, LA. Retrieved from http://digital.library.shsu.edu/cdm/search/searchterm/ audio-mp3/field/format/mode/all/conn/and/order/title/ad/asc

Memories of Terrebonne. Oral history archives. Retrieved from http://www.rootsweb.ancestry.com/ ~laterreb/tgs/memories.htm

Newton Gresham Library Digital Collections. Retrieved from http://cdm2635-01.cdmhost.com/ cdm/landingpage/collection/p243tutorial

Pitre descendants. Retrieved from https://www.facebook.com/groups/2423839222/

Remember Chauvin and Little Caillou when we were growing up. Retrieved fr om https://www.facebook.com/groups/247856658588347/

Robichaux, A. J., Jr. *Louisiana Census and Militia Lists 1770-1789*. Louisiana: Hebert Publications.

Robichaux, A. J., Jr. *The Acadian Exiles in Chattellerault 1773-1785*. Louisiana: Hebert Publications.

Robichaux, A. J., Jr. *The Acadian Exiles in Nantes 1775-1785*. Louisiana: Hebert Publications.

Robichaux, A. J., Jr. *The Acadian Exiles in Saint Malo 1758-1785*. Louisiana: Hebert Publications.

Social Security Death Master file. Retrieved from http://ssdmf.info/

St Joseph Catholic Church. Retrieved from http://www.stjosephchauvin.parishesonline.com/scripts/HostedSites/Org.asp?ID=15973

Taillandier. Retrieved from http://fr.wikipedia.org/wiki/Taillandier

Terrebonne Genealogical Society. Retrived from http://www.rootsweb.ancestry.com/~laterreb/tgs/

The hurricane of 1893. Retrieved from http://www.loyno.edu/~kchopin/new/culture/cheniere.html

The Louisiana Digital Library. Retrieved from http://louisdl.louislibraries.org/cdm/search/collection/LHP/searchterm/grand%20isle/order/nosort

The New Acadia project. Retrieved from http://www.ucs.louisiana.edu/~mar4160/nap.html

Windows into Yesteryears. Retrieved from https://www.facebook.com/groups/589475117806384/

INDEX

1763 Les Acadiens Deportes en Angleterre		
Duke Williams		
Le Bon Papa	http://froux.pagesperso-orange.fr/divers/bonpapa.htm	
L'Amite	A 400 ton ship led by Captain Joseph Beitremieux. Left France on August 20, 1785. 80 days later arrived on November 8, 1785. 270 people in 68 families. 6 deaths. http://froux.pagesperso-orange.fr/divers/amitie.htm	
	Marie Moyse age 45, widow of Olivier Pitre	Louis Constant Pitre son age 10; Victorie Pitre daughter age 19, Francoise Pitre daughter age 14
	Ursule Braud age 45, widow of Francois Pitre	Ursule Pitre daughter age 22
	Marguerite Boudrot age 46, widow of Benjamin Pitre	Marie Pitre daughter age 21, Magdelaine Pitre daughter age 12, Cecile Pitre daughter age 15, Maguerite Pitre daughter age 14, Etienne Pitre son age 7, Jean Pitre son age 4
	Joseph Pitre age 22 carpenter	Marie Hebert age 17, Joseph Hebert brother age 15
La Bergere	http://froux.pagesperso-orange.fr/divers/bergere.htm	
	Agnes Pitre (wife of Joseph Guerin)	
	Elisabeth Pitre (wife of Prospere Landry)	
	Natalie Pitre (widow of Jean Jacques Leblanc)	
	Amand Pitre (widower Genevieve Arsement)	and one daughter
	Marie Victoire Pitre (wife of Louis Ambroise Dugas)	
	Tranquille Pitre,	wife Elisabeth Aucoin, sons Jean Baptiste Pitre & Jean Vincent Pitre
	Ambroise Pitre	wife Elisabeth Dugas, sons Paul Ambroise Pitre & Jean Marie Pitre, and one daughter)
Le Beaumont		
La Ville d'Archangel		
	Marie Pitre, sa fille 16	
	Susanne Pitre (wife of Pierre Hebert)	
	Charles Pitre	wife Anne Henry, son Joseph Pitre & two daughters
	Jean Baptiste Pitre	wife Felicite Daigre, sons Pierre Pitre Jacques Pitre, Francois Pitre, and three daughters
	Marie Richard (widow Claude Pitre)	one daughter
Le Saint Remi	http://froux.pagesperso-orange.fr/divers/stremi.htm	
	Pierre Olivier Pitre	wife Rosalie Hebert, son Pierre Pitre and 3 daughters
	Anne Josephe Pitre (wife of Joseph Gautrot)	
	Marie Blanche Pitre (wife of Jerome Guerin)	
	Anselme Pitre, (widower Madeleine Leblanc)	son Jean Pierre Pitre & 3 daughters
La Caroline	http://froux.pagesperso-orange.fr/divers/caroline.htm	
	Martin Benonie Pitre	Pitre (and 2 half-siblings)

Index of Census

Year: 1850; Census Place: Barataria, Jefferson, Louisiana; Roll: M432_232; Page: 67A; Lines 16-22; Image: 138.

Year: *1860*; Census Place: *Ward 8, Terrebonne, Louisiana*; Roll: *M653_425*; Page: *73, Line 2-9*; Image: *401*; Family History Library Film: *803425*.

Year: *1880*; Census Place: *6th Ward, Terrebonne, Louisiana*; Roll: *472*; Family History Film: *1254472*; Page: *316B; Lines 9-14*; Enumeration District: *190*; Image: *0637*.

Year: *1910*; Census Place: *Police Jury Ward 6, Terrebonne, Louisiana*; Roll: *T624_529*; Page: *10A; Lines 21-31*; Enumeration District: *0108*; FHL microfilm: *1374542*.

Estimated based on Census & Genealogy Data, including partial and extrapolated lists	
(may include significant error rate, further research pending)	
United States	
Census Year	Pitre Descendants
1800	20
1810	20
1820	40
1830	80
1840	100
1850	180
1860	225
1870	150
1880	400
1890	600
1900	1,000
1910	1,300
1920	1,700
1930	2,000
1940	2,300
World Wide	
2010	800,000

Index of Churches

Saint John the Baptist Church at Dugas Cemetery, south of Montegut LA, built 1868 under direction of Father Jean Marie Joseph Denece. Destroyed in storm of 1909

Saint Joseph Catholic Church, Chauvin LA, 1842

Sacred Heart of Jesus built 1911, Montegut LA, under direction of Father Joseph Quenoulerie

Index of Individuals

Index of Place Names

Index of Water Ways

Table of Figures

Conveyancing records

1811 (07/12/1811) Marguerite Marie (Boudrot) Pitre's Spanish land grant

ARMAND FREMIN sells to ETIENNE PELTIER for $1200.00, a tract of land containing 3 arpents, 21 toises, 3 feet front by 40 arpents dept, located on the left bank of Bayou LaFourche, about 8 leagues below the Mississippi River, bounded above by Benjamin Baudreau, below by Laurent Fremin, acquired on 24 September 1806 from Widow Pitre, his mother-in-law. On 21 April 1813, Pierre Hebert, acting for Armand Philip Fremin, gives full acquittance.

1844 (06/13/1844)[47] Daniel Nettleton, Land conveyance record

LaFourche Township 17-S, Range 21-E, Section 7, 49.8 acres
Land purchased signed by "Daniel Nettleton"

---

[47] Nettleton Land http://search.ancestry.com/cgi-bin/sse.dll?db=BLMlandpatents&h=770855&indiv=try&o_vc=Record:OtherRecord&tid=877643&tpid=1228015363&rhSource=3550

RECORDS: BIRTH, BAPTISMS, MARRIAGE, DEATH, DRAFT

9/12/1918 Draft card – Élie Joseph Pitre, blue eyes, Montegut LA, 20 years old, born Feb 8, 1898, Deck Hand (employer Laurence F Hebert, 127 Brooklyn Ave, Houma LA

WWI registration records: Forest Joseph Pitre; Terrebonne, LA; born 3 Jan 1883; Bertha Breaux Pitre; tall height, stout build; grey eyes & dark hair.

Elesse Random Pitre: Ellis Randal Pitre; Terrebonne, LA; born 8 Feb 1885; Camelia White; medium height, medium build; brown eyes & brown hair.

Mrs. Élie (Cornelia White) Pitre Died April 29, 1934 in Montegut, Louisiana USA. She was 82 years old and was buried in Montegut on April 30, 1934.... Élie and Cornelia had 8 children, Annie married to Claude Naquin, Cordelia married to Ludgar J. Rhodes, Forrest, Johnny, Peter, Élie, Ellis.

Emily (Pitre) Long, 89, native of Houma, resident of Chauvin, died Sun., Sept. 12, 1993. Services at St. Joseph Catholic Church, burial in Saint Joseph Cemetery. Survived by son, Harry Long of Brownsville, TX; daughters, Emeline Cunningham and Dorothy Long, both of Chauvin; sisters, Rosanna Robichaux and Francis LeBouef, both of Montegut, Eldora Kieff of Houma, Cornelia Portier of Chauvin and Margarette Rome of Kenner; 10 grandchildren.; 12 great grandchildren.; and 2 great great grandchildren. Preceded by husband, Charles Dennis Long; parents, John Pitre Sr. and Francis Autin Pitre; son, Charles R. Long; brothers, Élie, Howard and Johnny Pitre; sisters, Lorena Pitre, Whisteria Carlos, America LeCompte and Anaise Savoie.

Marie Wisteria (Pitre) Carlos, 87, native of Montegut, resident of Chauvin, died at 2:05 a.m. today, June 26, 1984. Visitation at the Knights of Columbus Hall in Chauvin. Services at 2 p.m. Wed. at St. Joseph Catholic Church, Chauvin. Burial in church cemetery. She is survived by daughters, Mrs. Rosalie C. LeBouef of Houma and Mrs. Angelo Roberts (Jeanette) Babin of Chauvin; sisters, Mrs. America LeCompte, Mrs. Emily Long, Mrs. Cornelia Portier and Mrs. Eldora Kieff, all of Chvin, Mrs. Rosanna Robichaux, Mrs. Frances LeBeouf both of Montegut, Mrs. Naise Savoie of Houma and Mrs. Marguerite Rome of New Orleans; 8 grandchildren; 32 great-grandchildren and 19 great-great-grandchildren. She was preceded in death by husband, James Eugene Carlos; parents, Mr. and Mrs. John Pitre; brothers, Howard, John and Élie Pite; 1 grandchild, 3 great-great-grandchildren. Chauvin Funeral of Houma is handling arrangements.

America (Pitre) LeCompte, 84, native of Montegut, resident of Chauvin, died at 11:59 pm Tuesday (Jan. 27, 1987). Visitation in Knights of Columbus Hall in Chauvin. Services at 3 pm in St. Joseph Catholic Church. Burial in church cemetery. She is survived by sons, Percy, Aubrey and Charles LeCompte of Chauvin, Chester LeCompte of Gray and Lester LeCompte of Houma; daughters, Mrs. Easton (Helen) SoudÉlier of Houma and Mrs. J. B. (Barbara) Breaux; sisters, Mrs. Emily Long of Chauvin, Mrs. Eldora Keefe of Little Caillou, Mrs. Marguerite Rome of Metairie, Mrs. Naise Saboie of Houma, Mrs. Frances LeBoeuf of Montegut, Mrs. Roseanna Robichaux of Montegut and Mrs. Cornelia Portier of Chauvin; 32 grandchildren; 56 great-grandchildren; and 15 great-great-grandchildren. She was peceded in death by husband, Ruffin LeCompte; parents, John and Frances Autin Pitre; son, Cyrus LeCompte; daughter, Dorothy LeCompte; brothers, Élie, Howard and John Pitre; sisters, Wisteria Carlos and Lirina Pitre. She was a parishioner of St. Joseph Catholic Church and member of the Ladies Altar Society and Ladies Auxiliary of the Veterans of Foreign War #9608. Chauvin Funeral Home handled arrangements.

Marie Anaise (Pitre) Savoie, 87, native of Terrebonne Parish, resident of Houma, died Friday, Apr. 9, 1993. Services at Chauvin Funeral Home Chapel, burial in St. Francis Cem. #2. She is survived by daughter, Mrs. Wilmer (Elaine) Babin of Houma; sisters, Mrs. Jerome (Margaret) Rome of Kenner, Mrs. Davidson (Eldora) Keefe of Houma, Mrs. Harry (Emily) Long, Mrs. Ernest (Carnelia) Portier of Chauvin, Mrs. Stanley (Rosena) Robichaux and Mrs. Norris "Boots" (Frances) Leboeuf of Montegut; 2 grandchildren; 5 great-grandchildren; and 1 great-grandchild. She was preceded by husband, Charles A. Savoie; parents, John and Frances Autin Pitre Sr.; brothers, John, Élie and Howard Pitre; and sisters, Mrs. Jim (Westeria "Nan") Carlos and Mrs. Ruffin (America) LeCompte. She was a parishioner of St. Francis de Sales Catholic Church.

Rose Anna (Pitre) Robichaux, 90, a native of Chauvin and resident of Montegut, died at 10:56 p.m. Tuesday, July 7, 1998. Visitation will be from 5 to 10 p.m. today and from 8 a.m. to funeral time Thursday, at the Montegut Fire Station. Mass will be at 11 a.m. Thursday at Sacred Heart Catholic Church, with burial in the church cemetery. She is survived by three sons, Druby J. Robichaux of Montegut, Robert P. Robichaux of Houma, and Wilbur W. Robichaux of Memphis, Tenn.; four sisters, Mrs. Davidson (Eldorah) Kieff of Montegut, Mrs. Norris (Frances) LeBoeuf of Bourg, Mrs. Ernest (Cornelia) Portier of Chauvin, and Mrs. Yank (Marguerite) Rome of Kenner; 12 grandchildren; and 20 great-grandchildren. She was preceded in death by her husband, Stanley William Robichaux; her parents, John J. and Frances Autin Pitre Sr.; three brothers, Élie, John and Howard Pitre; and five sisters, Mrs. James (Witeria) Carlos, Mrs. Harry (Emily) Long, Mrs. Ruffin (America) Lecompte, Mrs. Charles (Anaize) Savoie and Lorena Pitre. She was a homemaker and a parishioner of Sacred Heart Catholic Church.

Eldora (Pitre) Keefe, 91, a native of Chauvin and resident of San Antonio, died at 1 a.m. Monday, April 26, 2004. Visitation will be from 5 to 10 p.m. today and from 8 a.m. to funeral time Friday at the Knights of Columbus Hall in Chauvin. Rosary will be recited at 7 p.m. today at the funeral home. Services will be at 10 a.m. Friday at St. Joseph Catholic Church, with burial in the church cemetery. She is survived by one daughter and son-in-law, Mary and Mike Brown; one stepdaughter, Gertrude Scott and husband, Alvin Scott Sr.; two sisters, Cornelia Portier and Margerite Rome; 11 grandchildren, Cindy Price, Lori Francis, Jennifer Gregoire, Julius Kieff Jr., David Kieff, Alvin Scott Jr., Enola Fanguy, Verna Layne, Alisa Frederick, Eric D. Thibodeaux and James C. Brown; numerous great-grandchildren; and two great-great-grandchildren. She was preceded in death by her husband, Davidson J. Keefe; her parents, John E. Pitre Sr. and Frances Autin Pitre; one stepson, Julius Kieff Sr.; three brothers, John Pitre Jr., Élie Pitre and Howard Pitre; and six sisters, Westeria Carlos, America LeCompte, Rosanna Robichaux, Emily Long, Anise Savoie and Francis LeBoeuf. In lieu of flowers, memorial donations may be made to St. Joseph Catholic Church. Chauvin Funeral Home is in charge of arrangements.

Frances (Pitre) LeBoeuf   A Mass of Christian burial will be celebrated at 2 p.m. Tuesday at Sacred Heart Church in Montegut for Frances Pitre LeBoeuf, 86, a native of Chauvin and resident of Bourg, who died Sept. 15, 2001. Visitation will be 9 a.m. until funeral time at the Montegut Fire Station. Burial will be at the church cemetery. She was the wife of Norris "Boots" G. LeBoeuf of Bourg; mother of Roberta "Bobbie" Duplantis of Bourg; and sister of Cornelia Portier, Eldora Keiffe and Marguerite Rome. She is also survived by three grandchildren and three great-grandchildren. She was preceded in death by her parents, John and Frances Autin Pitre; son, Vernon Paul LeBoeuf; brothers, Ellie, Howard and John Pitre; sisters, Wisteria Carlos, America LeCompte, Anise Savoie, Emily Long and Roseanna Robichaux; and grandson, Kelly Duplantis. She was Catholic. Samart Funeral Home and Crematorium of Houma is in charge of arrangements.

Cornelia Pitre: Lafourche Daily Comet, Thursday, 20 May 2010: Cornelia Pitre Portier, 90, a native of Chauvin and resident of Houma, died at 9:10 p.m. Tuesday, May 18, 2010. Visitation will be from 9:30 a.m. to funeral time Friday at St. Joseph Catholic Church in Chauvin. Mass will be 11:30 a.m. Friday at the church, with burial in the church cemetery. She is survived by one daughter, Gladys P. Price and husband, Charles Sr. of Chauvin; one son, Renauld Joseph Portier of Houma; six grandchildren; nine great-grandchildren; five great-great-grandchildren and one expected in October; one step-great-grandchild; and one step-great-great-grandchild. She was preceded in death by her husband, Earnest Portier Jr.; her parents, John Pitre Sr. and Marie Francis Autin Pitre; one son, Richard Paul Portier; three brothers, John Pitre Jr., Élie Pitre and Howard Pitre; and eight sisters, Margerite Rome, Westeria Carlos, America LeCompte, Rosanna Robichaux, Emily Long, Anise Savoie, Francis LeBoeuf and Eldora Keefe. She was a parishioner of St. Joseph Catholic Church and a homemaker. She enjoyed gardening and loved her flowers. She loved her children and grandchildren very much. She was very fortunate to have seen and loved the fifth generation of her family. Her family would like to thank Heritage Manor of Houma for all the care and generosity they have given throughout the past three years. Chauvin Funeral Home is in charge of arrangements.

John Pitre Jr funeral services were held, Saturday, march 11, at 9 am for John Pitre Jr., 44, from his home at Chauvin to St Jon's Catholic Church. The deceased is survived by his wife, the former Aline Prosperie, one son, Cyrun and two daughters, Lucy Mae and Carolyn Marie, one brother Élie Pitre of Delcambre and the following sisters: Mrs Morris LeBoeuf, Mrs Stanley Robichaux, Montegut; Mrs Albert Pitre, New Orleans; Mrs Charley Savoie, Houma; Mesdames Ruffin LeCompte, C.D. Long, James Carlos, Ernest Portier and Davidson Kleffe, all of Chauvin. Pitre was a lifelong resident of Terrebonne Parish. He was a member of Knights of Columbus and of the Holy Name Society of St Joseph's Church. He was a diesel mechanic by profession. Interment was in the St Joseph's catholic cemetery, Chauvin.

Élie Joseph Pitre A ship builder and a resident of 500 Pitre St., Delcambre, LA. Died in Erath LA June 24, 1978 at 10pm at age fo 80. Visitation at the Knights of Columbus Home in Chauvin preceded the funeral at St Joseph Church in Chauvin LA, which was held at 10am followed by interment in the church cemetery. He si survived by two sons, Wilbert J. of Delcambre and Lee Roy J of Lafayette; one daughter, Mrs V.J. (Doris) Malbrough of Houma; nine sisters, Mrs James Carlos, Mrs Ruffin LeCompte, Mrs Harry Long, Mrs Ernest Portier and Mrs Davidson Keiff, all of Chauvin, Mrs Norris LeBouef and Mrs Stanley Robichaux both of Montegut, Mrs Charlie Savoie of Houma and Mrs Thomas Rorne of Kenner. The was preceded in death by his wife Leona LeBouef and two brothers Howard and Johnny Pitre Jr. Arrangements are begin handed by Chauvin Funeral Home.

Wilbert James Pitre: Houma Courier, 1 April 2006: Wilbert James Pitre, 83, a native of Chauvin and longtime resident of Delcambre, died at 1:15 a.m. Thursday, March 30, 2006, at his residence surrounded by his loved ones. Visitation will be from noon until 10 p.m. Sunday with a rosary at 7 p.m., and from 8 a.m. until funeral time Monday at Evangeline Funeral Home in New Iberia. A funeral will be at 2 p.m. Monday at Our Lady of the Lake Catholic Church with the Rev. Herb Bennerfeild officiating. Interment will follow at Our Lady of the Lake Mausoleum. He is survived by his wife of 64 years, Hilda Boudelouche Pitre of Delcambre; one son, Bryan Pitre Sr. and wife, Sandra, of Delcambre; one brother, LeRoy Pitre, of Lafayette; one daughter-in-law, Ruth Pitre, of Delcambre; five grandchildren, Mary LeBlanc and husband, Kerry, of New Iberia, Bryan Pitre Jr. and wife, Janet, Zachary Pitre and wife, Buffy, Stacie Pommier and husband, Carl, and Patrick Pitre, all of Delcambre; seven great-grandchildren, Len Monceaux and wife, Lena, Austin Sonnier, Trevor Pitre, Adam Pitre and Jayce Pitre, all of Delcambre, Misty LeBlanc of Broussard, and Cheramie Pitre of Dodson; three great-great-grandchildren, Kelsea Monceaux, Braie Monceaux and David Monceaux, all of Delcambre; and numerous nieces and nephews. He was preceded in death by his parents, Élie and Leona LeBouef Pitre; one son, David J. Pitre Sr.; one grandson, David J. Pitre Jr.; and one sister, Doris Malbrough. He was a respected boat builder in several parishes until he started his own business in Delcambre, Pitre Shipyard. He enjoyed fishing and hunting, but most of all he loved spending time with his family. He was a parishioner of Our Lady of the Lake Catholic Church where he was an usher and passed the collection. Pallbearers will be Bryan Pitre Jr., Carl Pommier, Zachary Pitre, Kerry LeBlanc, Len Monceaux, Patrick Pitre and Austin Sonnier. Honorary pallbearers will be Trevor Pitre, Adam Pitre and David Monceaux. Evangeline Funeral Home is in charge of arrangements.

Lee Roy James Pitre, Sr. Funeral Services were held Monday, October 16, 2006 at a 10:00 AM Service in La Chapelle de Martin & Castille for Lee Roy J. Pitre, Sr. age 78, who passed away Saturday, October 14, 2006 at Southwest Medical Center.Interment will be in Fountain Memorial Gardens Cemetery.Reverend Jerry Mesley, Associate Pastor of St. Edmond Catholic Church will conduct the Funeral Services. Survivors include his loving wife of 46 years, Lou T. Pitre of Lafayette; three sons, Lee Roy Pitre, Jr. and his wife, Lilia of Lafayette, Jarvis Pitre and his wife, Tammy of Lafayette and Eric Pitre and his wife, Laura of Frisco, Texas; nine grandchildren, Desiree' Pitre and her husband, Mark, Elizabeth Pitre, Stephanie Pitre, Dilyara and Jana Emiraliyeva, Daniel Pitre, Matthew Pitre, Nathan Pitre and Cohn Pitre and two great grandchildren, Jacob and Victoria Sehedler. He was preceded in death by his parents, Elie Joseph Pitre and the former, Leona LeBouef; one brother, Wilbert Joseph Pitre; one sister, Doris Malbrough and one granddaughter, Emily Pitre.A native of Chauvin, Louisiana and a resident of Lafayette for sixty six years, Mr. Pitre was a veteran of military service, having served in the United States Army. He was a retired carpenter, specializing in cabinetry and worked as a supervisor for over twenty five years with Dwight Andrus Home Builders. Prior to that, he built shrimp boats, starting at a very young age with his father. Mr. Pitre extremely enjoyed the outdoors and his favorite hobbies were fishing, hunting, shrimping and crabbing. A Rosary will be prayed Sunday at 7:00 PM in the Martin & Castille Funeral Home in Lafayette. The family requests that visiting hours be observed Sunday from 10:00 AM until 9:00 PM and Monday from 8:00 AM until time of service. Pallbearers will be Lee Roy Pitre, Jr., Jarvis Pitre, Eric Pitre, Shane Trahan, John Traschel, and James Williams.

GLOSSARY

Teche is an Indian word meaning "snake."

Bayou LaFourche at 106 miles long, it is known as the "longest street in the world." Originally called Chetimachas River. The name is French for fork.

"Bogalusa" is derived from the Indian named creek "Bogue Lusa," which flows through the city.

The world famous **Mardi Gras** holiday is celebrated throughout south-central and southwestern Louisiana in an ancient custom that originated in southern Europe. It celebrates food and fun just before the 40 days of Lent – a Catholic tradition of prayer and sacrifice.

Marais Carlin (Carlin Pond) and Grand Marais (Big Pond) – Delcambre, Louisiana

Chauvin's Lagniappe--a Cajun-Spanish word for "a little extra free something,"

Chipoudy – Present day Hopewell Hill near Shepody, New Brunswick, was an Acadian village that was founded in 1698 by Pierre Thibaudeau. It was destroyed in 1755 by English soldiers attempting to deport the Acadians.

Cobequid – derived from the Mi'kmaq word "Wagobagitk" roughly translated as "the bay runs far up". Mathieu Martin was given Cobequid as a land grant in 1689. He was the first Acadian born in Acadia. The area now called Masstown near Truro was formerly a primary farming community.

Cordele - a heavy twisted rope for towing boats

Daigeville is a small rural community south of Houma about 1 mile north of Chauvin along west side of bayou.

Grand Pre - (Big Meadow)

La Fourche des Chétimachas – Name applied early by French settlers during late 1600s due to a small Indian village occupied by the Chétimachas tribe located near the junction of Bayou LaFourche and the Mississippi river.

Les Mines – was an Acadian village in the Minas Basin. It was destroyed in 1755 during the deportation.

Petit Manchac (also Grand Praire and Vermilionville) – Lafayette

Pisiguit – (Now Windsor) from the Mi'kmaq term *Pesaquid* meaning "Junction of Waters".

Pont du Beaux – Breaux Bridge. In 1799 Firmin Breaux build a footbridge across the Bayou Teche for his family and neighbors. When travelers would ask for directions, they would sometimes be told to go to Breaux's Bridge. This was eventually adopted as the city's name.

Terrebonne Parish was created on March 22, 1822 from La Fourche Parish. The parish was named for the French phrase" terre bonne" or in English, good earth.

Acadiana is a "Cajun Country," the popular term given to an eight-parish region.
Lafayette Parish is at the heart of Acadiana and is surrounded by the remaining seven parishes: Acadia, Evangeline, Iberia, Saint Landry, Saint Martin, Saint Mary, and Vermilion. (Unlike other states, Louisiana has parishes rather than counties.)

Andouille (ahn-do-ee) is a spicy country sausage used in Gumbo and other Cajun dishes.

Apothecary (*ah-POTH-i-kerry*) is a historical name for a medical practitioner who formulates and dispenses materials to physicians, surgeons and patients — a role now served by a pharmacist.

Bay of Fundy (French: *Baie de Fundy*) is a bay located on the Atlantic coast of North America, on the northeast end of the Gulf of Maine between the Canadian provinces of New Brunswick and Nova Scotia, with a small portion touching the U.S. state of Maine. The Bay of Fundy is known for having the greatest difference in water level between its high and low tides in the world. The name "Fundy" is thought to date back to the 16th century when the Portuguese referred to the bay as "Rio Fundo" or "deep river".

Bayou (bi-yoo) is the stream; there are numerous bayous crisscrossing Louisiana.

Bayou \BUY-you\n. is also a French name for slow moving river.

Beignet (ben-yea) Delicious sweet doughnuts, square-shaped and minus the hole, lavishly sprinkled with powdered sugar. Sometimes served with coffee au lait (coffee with chicory and milk).

Bisque (bis-k) - a thick, cream or milk-based shellfish soup, usually made with crawfish, shrimp or oysters.

Bon Appetite! (bon a-pet-tite') Good appetite - or "Enjoy!"

Boucherie (boo-shuh-ree) is a community butchering which involves several families contributing the animal(s) -- usually pigs -- to be slaughtered. Each family helps to process the different cuts of meat, like sausage, ham, boudin, chaudin, chops, and head cheese. Each family gets to take home their share of the yield. This process was done in late fall to provide meat throughout the cold months.

Boudin (boo-dan) is hot, spicy pork mixed with onions, cooked rice, herbs, and stuffed in sausage casing.

Bourre (boo-ray) is French for "stuffed." It is the name of a Cajun card game which requires the loser of a hand to stuff the pot with chips.

Cafu Lait (kah-fay-oh-lay) Coffee with steamed milk.

Cajun (cay-jun) is slang for Acadians, the French-speaking people who migrated to South Louisiana from Nova Scotia in the eighteenth century. Cajuns were happily removed from city life preferring a rustic life along the bayous. The term now applies to the people, the culture, and the cooking.   A person of French Canadian descent born or living along the bayous, marshes, and prairies of southern Louisiana. The word Cajun began in 19th century Acadie (now Nova Scotia, Canada) when the Acadians began to arrive. The French of noble ancestry would say, "les Acadiens", while some referred to the Acadians
as "le 'Cadiens", dropping the "A". Later came the Americans who could not pronounce "Acadien" or "'Cadien", so the word "Cajun" was born.

Cayenne (ki-yan) is hot pepper that is dried and used to season many Louisiana dishes.

Chicory (chick-ory) is an herb, the roots of which are dried, ground; roasted and used to flavor coffee.

Coonass (koon-ass) is a controversial term in the Cajun lexicon: to some Cajuns it is regarded as the supreme ethnic slur, meaning "ignorant, backwards Cajun"; to others the term is a badge of. In South Louisiana, for example, one can often see bumper stickers reading "Registered Louisiana Coonass". The word originated in South Louisiana, and is derived from the belief that Cajuns frequently ate raccoons. It is proposed that the term contains a negative racial connotation: namely, that Cajuns were "beneath" or "under" blacks (or coons, as blacks were often called by racists).

Couche-Couche (koosh-koosh) is a popular breakfast food, made by frying cornmeal and topping it with milk and/or cane syrup.

Courtbouillon (coo-boo-yon) is a rich, spicy tomato-based soup or stew made with fish fillets, onions, and sometimes mixed vegetables.

Crawfish (craw-fish), sometimes spelled "crayfish," resemble lobsters, but are much smaller. Locally, they are known as "mudbugs," because they live and grow in the mud of freshwater bayous. They can be served many ways: in etouffees, jambalaya, gumbo, or simply boiled.

Creole (cree-ol) is the word that originally described those people of mixed French and Spanish blood who migrated from Europe or were born in Southeast Louisiana and lived as sophisticated city or plantation dwellers. The term has expanded and now embraces a type of cuisine and a style of architecture.

Dirty Rice is a pan-fried leftover cooked rice sautéed with green peppers, onion, celery, stock, liver, giblets and many other ingredients.

Etoufee (ay-too-fay) is a succulent, tangy tomato-based sauce. A smothered dish usually made with crawfish or shrimp. Crawfish and shrimp etouffees are New Orleans and Cajun country specialties.

Fais do do (fay-doe-doe) is a name for the party where traditional Cajun dance is performed. This phrase literally means "to make sleep," although the parties are the liveliest of occasions with food, music, and dancing.

File (fee-lay) Ground sassafras leaves used to season, among other things, gumbo.

Flemish is an adjective from Flanders, a medieval country in Western Europe, extending along the North Sea from the Strait of Dover to the Scheldt River: the corresponding modern regions include the provinces of East Flanders and West Flanders in West Belgium, and the adjacent parts of N France and SW Netherlands.

A historical region of northwest Europe including parts of northern France, western Belgium, and southwest Netherlands along the North Sea. For many centuries it enjoyed virtual independence and great prosperity as a center of the cloth industry. The Hapsburg wars in the Low Countries caused the eventual division of the region, which suffered heavy damage during both World Wars.
A Dutch-speaking region of northern Belgium. It was granted limited autonomy in 1980.

Fricassee (free-kay-say) is a stew made by browning then removing meat from the pan, making a roux with the pan drippings, and then returning meat to simmer in the thick gravy.

Gumbo (gum-boe) is a thick, robust roux-based soup sometimes thickened with okra or file'. There are thousands of variations, such as shrimp or seafood gumbo, chicken or duck gumbo, okra and file' gumbo.

Jambalaya (jum-bo-lie-yah). Louisiana chefs "sweep up the kitchen" and toss just about everything into the pot. A rice dish with any combination of beef, pork, fowl, smoked sausage, ham, or seafood, as well as celery, green peppers and often tomatoes.

Joie de Vivre (zhwa-d-veev) is an attitude towards life

King Cake is a ring shaped oval pastry, decorated with colored sugar in the traditional Mardi Gras colors, purple, green, and gold, which represent justice, faith, and power. A small plastic baby is hidden inside the cake. Tradition requires that the person who gets the baby in their piece must provide the next King Cake.

Lagniappe (lan-yap) is a Cajun word for "something extra," like the extra donut in a baker's dozen; an unexpected nice surprise.

Laissez les bon temps rouler (lay-zay lay bon ton rule-ay) – Let the good times roll!

Levee (le-vee) is an embankment built to keep a river from overflowing; a landing place on the river.

Maque Chou (mock-shoo) is a dish made by scraping young corn off the cob and smothering the kernels in tomatoes, onion, and spices.

Mardi Gras (mardi graw) commonly known as Fat Tuesday, it is the day before Ash Wednesday, the first day of the Roman Catholic season of Lent. It's also the day of the Biggest Party on Earth!

Pain Perdu (pan-pear-doo) means "lost bread"; a breakfast treat made by soaking stale bread in an egg batter, then frying and topping with cane syrup or powdered sugar.

Pirogue (pee-row) is a Cajun canoe.

Po-Boy is a sandwich extravaganza that began as a five-cent lunch for poor boys. Always made with French bread, po-boys can be stuffed with fried oysters, shrimp, fish, crawfish, meatballs, smoked sausage and more.

Praline (praw-leen) is the sweetest of sweets, this New Orleans tradition is a candy patty made of sugar, cream and pecans.

Red Beans & Rice is the traditional Monday meal in New Orleans, red beans are cooked with ham or sausage and seasonings, and served over rice.

Roux (rue) is a base of gumbos or stews, made of flour and oil mixture.

Sauce Piquante (saws-pee-kawnt) means "spicy sauce"; is a spicy stew.

Tasso (tah-soh) are strips of spiced pork or beef which are smoked like jerky and used to flavor many dishes; a sort of Cajun pepperoni.

Taillandier [male name] (to cut) is a manufacturer of articles of edge-tool industry.

Vieux Carre (voo ca-ray) is a French phrase meaning "old quarter" and referring to the French Quarter.

Zydeco (zi-de-co) is a relatively new kind of Cajun dance music that is a combination of traditional Cajun dance music, R&B, and African blues

Valenzuela is an area in Louisiana along the left bank of the Bayou LaFourche where it merged with the Mississippi River, between present day Donaldsonville and Plattenville. Initially settled in the late 1700's under Spanish rule, as a result of the Canary Island immigration. This area was also referred to as the second Acadian coast.

Lagniappe

Louisiana is named in honor of King Louis XIV. The French were the first European nation to establish permanent settlements in territory. In 1803 the United States paid France $15 million for the Louisiana Territory. The deal included all lands drained by the Mississippi river. Louisiana has Parishes instead of Counties. Originally there were church units set up by the Spanish provisional governor in 1669. Louisiana is also the only state that is based on the Napoleonic code. Louisiana leads the nation in the production of. About half of the production comes from the Atchafalaya Basin and half from an aquaculture system consisting of thousands of acres of ponds throughout the state.

A Short Tour around Louisiana

Abbeville was founded in 1843 and named after the founder's hometown in France. For more detailed information visit www.vermilion.org/abbeville.php.

Baton Rouge ("Red Stick" translated from French) is a capital of Louisiana. It is considered to be the second largest city in Louisiana after New Orleans. For more detailed information visit http://brgov.com/.

Breaux Bridge is known as "The Crawfish Capital of the World". In 1771, an Acadian pioneer Firmin Breaux began buying up. In 1799 Breaux built a footbridge across the Bayou Teche. This first bridge was a suspension bridge. Eventually, "Breaux's Bridge" was adopted as the city's name. For more detailed information visit www.breauxbridgelive.com/.

Chauvin is mostly a quiet bayou community located south of along the Bayou Petit Caillou. The "Blessing of the Fleet" during most shrimp festivals originated from this little town in the late 1920's and was first known as "boat blessing". For more detailed information visit www.idcide.com/citydata/la/chauvin.htm.

Delcambre is a small town located on the boundary of Iberia and Vermilion parishes. It's located about twelve miles east of Abbeville on Louisiana Highway 14. It was first settled by Acadians from Nova Scotia in the mid-18th century. Delcambre canal also known as Bayou Carlin, runs from Lake Peigneur to the Vermilion Bay. For more detailed information visit www.vermilion.org/delcambre.php

Gueydan is known as "The Duck Capital of America" in recognition of its abundance of waterfowl. For more detailed information visit www.gueydan.org/.

Houma was founded in 1810 and incorporated in 1848. The name was derived from the Houmas Indian tribe. Houma and the surrounding communities are steeped deep in Cajun tradition and culture. For more detailed information visit www.houmalouisiana.com/.

Jean Lafitte – The town of Jean Lafitte was once a thriving community of pirates. It is a Cajun fishing village and tourist spot on Bayou Barataria in Jefferson Parish. It is named after the owner Jean Lafitte. For more detailed information visit www.nps.gov/jela/.

[Reword…] Lafayette (Vermillionville). Around the mid-1700s, French speaking Acadians settled this region of south Louisiana. The Acadians were joined by other settlers referred to as Creoles. During this time, Louisiana area was under Spanish rule and new settlers were greatly welcomed and sought after. Lafayette is a city nestled along the winding Vermilion River. The city was originally founded as Vermilionville in 1821 by an Acadian named Jean Mouton. Tin 1884, it was renamed for the Marquis de Lafayette, who assisted the United States during the Revolutionary War. Lafayette is considered to be the heart of French Louisiana. It is famous for authentic Cajun cuisine, Zydeco and Cajun music, scenic swamplands, Acadian Village, Vermilionville, Acadian Cultural Center, and much more. The city's economy was primarily based on agriculture until the 1940s when the petroleum and natural gas industry became dominant. It has one of the highest restaurant counts per capital of cities in the area "Lafayette Convention and Visitors Commission (www.lafayettetravel.com)" For more detailed information visit www.lafayettela.gov/

Morgan City was originally known as Tigre Island because of the spotting of an unknown cat by U.S surveyors. The area was settled by a Kentucky planter and surgeon Walter Brashear. The Attakapas Indians called it Atchafalaya or "long river". During 1917, the first Tarzan movie starring Elmo. The Louisiana Shrimp and Petroleum Festival, held in Morgan City, is the oldest state-chartered harvest festival, established on Labor Day 1936. For more detailed information visit www.cityofmc.com/

Natchitoches (pronounced Nack-a-tish, a Natchitoches Indian word meaning "place of the Paw Paw", or "Chinquapin") is the oldest permanent settlement in Louisiana. Natchitoches was established in 1714 by Louis Juchereau de St. Denis. It was originally founded as an outpost by the French on the Red River to trade with the Spanish in Mexico and played a major role in the history of Texas and Louisiana. For more detailed information visit www.natchitoches.com/.

New Orleans is commonly known as "The Big Easy" or "The Crescent City". La Nouvelle-Orléans was founded in 1718 by the French Mississippi Company under the direction of Jean-Baptiste Le Moyne de Bienville. It is named after Philippe II, Duke of Orleans and Regent of France. For more detailed information visit www.cityofno.com/.

Opelousas lays claim to being the third oldest city in Louisiana. The present location of the city began development around 1720 when French trappers began settling in the area. They were followed by French missionaries trying to evangelize the Indians. The city of Opelousas is situated at the juncture of Interstate 49 and US Highway 190. Although, its name has been given many meanings, it's long been accepted as "Black leg." This is due to the belief that members of the tribe painted their legs a dark color. The tribe lived just west of two small lakes east of Opelousas. This is considered to be the westernmost channel of the prehistoric Mississippi river. Jim Bowie lived in Opelousas after moving there from Kentucky. For more detailed information visit www.cityofopelousas.com/

Rayne is known as "The Frog Capital of the World". For more detailed information visit www.rayne.org/index.htm, or www.exploratorium.edu/frogs/rayne/index.html.

Saint Francisville was incorporated in 1813 under the Lawrason Act. For more detailed information visit www.stfrancisville.net/.

Saint Martinville is the third oldest town in Louisiana and is located on the Bayou Teche approximately sixteen miles south of Breaux Bridge and eighteen miles southeast of Lafayette. It is also the site of the Evangeline Oak made famous in Longfellow's poem. For more detailed information visit www.stmartinparish-la.org/

Thibodaux is located in on Bayou LaFourche. Established in 1801 by Henry Schuyler Thibodaux. For more detailed information visit www.ci.thibodaux.la.us/.

Vermillionville See Lafayette.

Figure 50 : Cornelia Mathilda (White) Pitre; 1st Row Dugas Cemetery

Figure 51 : Francis Marie (Autin) Pitre;

1st Row St Joseph cemetery

Figure 52 : John Pitre;

1st Row St Joseph Cemetery;

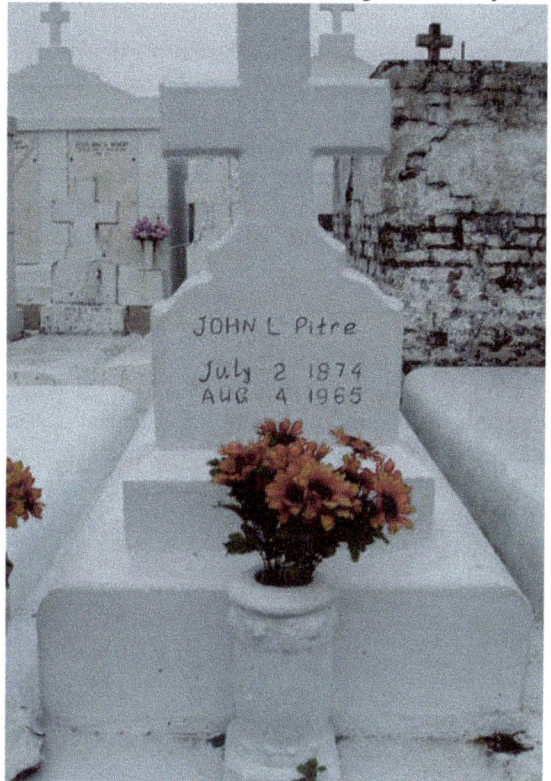

Cajun vs Creole cuisine

Some people not familiar with the culture think that Cajuns are lazy and live to eat. This could not be further from the truth. Cajuns are hardworking creative people. However, family and enjoying life are far more important. Over time, distinctions outside Louisiana between Cajun and Creole cuisine and culture have been blurred. However, there are significant differences. Creole dishes tend to be more continental, although using local produce. Cajun food is cooked at higher temperatures for longer with more seasoning, sometimes spicy, and tends to be heartier. Many well-known Cajun dishes were originally centered on wild game, rice, and other local ingredients, cooked in a large cast iron pot over a large open fire.

Festivals

Laissez les bons temps rouler, is a cliché which originated from local culture. It is rather easily translated as meaning "let the good times roll." Nearly every village, town, and city of any size has a yearly festival, celebrating an important part of the local economy. The majority of Cajun festivals include live music, local dances and plenty of local dishes.

www.ingramcontent.com/pod-product-compliance
Lightning Source LLC
Chambersburg PA
CBHW080250030426
42334CB00023BA/2763